YOU CAN'T SEE MY SCARS

A Story of Thriving During the Impossible
and Living Life to the Fullest

Darren Cosentino

Sara Cosentino

 FriesenPress

Suite 300 - 990 Fort St
Victoria, BC, V8V 3K2
Canada

www.friesenpress.com

ISBN
978-1-5255-0886-8 (Hardcover)
978-1-5255-0887-5 (Paperback)
978-1-5255-0888-2 (eBook)

1. BIOGRAPHY & AUTOBIOGRAPHY, PERSONAL MEMOIRS

Distributed to the trade by The Ingram Book Company

Table of Contents

FOREWORD

CANCER: That dreaded word that strikes terror in the hearts of so many people in our world today has been, unfortunately, all too familiar a topic in our family. My father died of pancreatic cancer in 1975 (in his case it was twelve weeks from diagnosis to death). The mother and maternal grandmother of my wife, Janice, both had their lives cut short by cancer. Our daughter, Allison, fought a courageous battle with melanoma for almost four years before succumbing to this disease in 2013.

When Janice was diagnosed with breast cancer at forty-five, we were devastated. I couldn't tell people about it without breaking into tears. Since I was Premier at the time, it had to be treated with great sensitivity. Janice did not want "special treatment." Fortunately for us, the wonderful professionals at Cancer Care Manitoba give special treatment to everyone who walks through their doors. The doctors, nurses, technicians, and support staff are gifted, professional, sensitive, caring, and dedicated to giving every patient the best advice, treatment, and support available.

Having a family member diagnosed with cancer is a constant emotional roller coaster. The sense of helplessness as you search for answers is profound, but the battle is fought every day by the patients. They live in that Neverland of dread, determination, and hope.

As I watched Janice go through her battle, I was in awe of her emotional strength. She had always been committed to a healthy lifestyle, but her positive attitude and her strong mental commitment to regaining her health was amazing. More than anything else, I believe it enabled her to survive.

As I learned about Darren's story from Sara, I saw so many parallels in his battle against cancer. His strength of character and will to live allowed him to turn a prognosis of six months to live into almost six years of remarkable life experiences, creating memories for his family, friends, and all those who became part of his story.

Darren challenged everyone, whether medical professionals or friends and observers, to believe that he could do so much more. He was not content to merely prolong his life, but determined to live with quality and purpose. His amazing physical accomplishments while battling for survival both impressed and inspired all those around him. His adventurous spirit and interest in the people he met along his journey are a unique and special story.

At heart, Darren was a storyteller who was comfortable in any setting, sharing his stories and gathering his fellow travelers into his inner circle. We can all learn and benefit from Darren's stories.

In particular, Darren's story can provide great encouragement for anyone who might get a cancer diagnosis. It teaches us that we are not limited merely by hope for a positive outcome, because with each passing year new discoveries and treatment options are being developed. More importantly, the human spirit and a positive attitude play a critical part in the outcome.

Honourable Gary Filmon, P.C., O.C., O.M., LLD

CHAPTER 1
A CHOICE: TO LIVE

Sara and Darren Cosentino

*"It's clear to me now that I will die of cancer.
That much has been decided for me...but I get to decide how I will live."*

- Darren Cosentino

When people see me for the first time they assume I'm a perfectly healthy and active forty-three-year-old man. There's no reason for them to think otherwise. I'm more active than eighty percent of my friends and I don't look like a person who has gone through forty-six rounds of chemo, multiple liver surgeries and resections, and sudden cardiac death. Twice. That is, until I take my shirt off and my scars are visible. I go to hot yoga five times a week and I swim in the lake every day during the summer. I paddleboard, fish, hunt, and travel. I live a life that most people dream of living once they retire. The only difference is that I was diagnosed with Stage 4 colon cancer and given six months to live in January of 2011.

This diagnosis is a death sentence. The unfortunate reality is that you don't beat the kind of cancer I have. Every day revolves around cancer, but that's not me. When I'm not in chemo or gearing up for a surgery, I don't have cancer. At least that's how my wife, Sara, and I have chosen to handle the cards we've been dealt. My diagnosis changed my life but I won't let it stop me from living.

The last five years of my life have been filled with what feels like a lifetime of wild adventure. My diagnosis gave Sara and me a reason to embrace life and celebrate every day we have together, whether hosting guests at our cottage or travelling during our weeks off chemo. While I've always been adventurous and active, cancer has made me even more ambitious. The only time you'll find me curled up watching a movie is during -30°C degree winter weather. If the sun is up, I'm on the go and often outside.

Throughout my treatments, we've experienced many little victories that have made our lives easier. These "wins" range from surgeries going off without a hitch to amazing doctors and nurses who genuinely care, friends who have become family, and last-minute chemo-free scuba diving vacations. Sara and I always keep our focus on the immediate situation and what actions we need to take in order to move forward. When you have Stage 4 cancer it's all about the next step to prolong your life. The doctors will do their best to eradicate as much cancer as possible but I know it will be the death of me. I just don't know when.

I wrote this book with the hope that my story would help people who find themselves in situations such as ours. I want the world to know that a shitty diagnosis doesn't have to keep you from living. It doesn't have to be the end. In recounting the amazing support I've received, I hope to help people better understand how to support loved ones during treatment. I also want to use this book to thank every person who has made my journey a little better along the way. This is not a dark or depressing story because we refuse to let it be. My story is full of humour, kindness, adventure, and life.

Before we head into the details, let me tell you a little about who I was prior to my diagnosis. As a kid I was very imaginative; I dressed up in my Superman costume whether it was Halloween or not. I'm an only child so I was always finding new ways to entertain myself. I have been extremely busy and involved in many different social scenes since I was very young. I thrived on the social aspect of activities like sports. You could always find me running laps at my elementary school—tackling the challenge to outrun every kid in my grade. This continued into my teenage life, when I ran my first half marathon at twelve years old. When I began high school, my strong Italian heritage led me to the soccer field, where I thrived, naturally. I also ran track and played volleyball but I was more into the social aspect and meeting girls than I was the actual sports.

I won the election for vice-president at Charleswood Junior High School by creating a rap that I used in my campaign. My rap skills were accompanied by some killer breakdancing moves that were a hit at every pre-teen dance club around town. I have to admit, I spent more time in the hallways of my school than I did in the classroom, but when I did apply myself, I passed my classes. I was always extremely respectful to my teachers and peers. When one of my classmates, who had a learning disability, was being picked on incessantly, I took a stand for him. From then on I made a special point of including him in activities and events. Sara would say I've always been compassionate and protective of those around me.

The value of hard work was instilled in me at a young age; I started working construction at eleven years old. I laid bricks for less than minimum wage because I was so young, but I worked hard and at times napped on the floor of the construction site after an exhausting day. By the end of that first summer my supervisor gave me a raise; he recognized that I contributed just as much as the adults on the crew. This recognition stuck with me and carried over into other fields of work. In high school, I sold books door to door and learned that I loved to sell. I realized I could make just as much money by chatting with strangers as I could working construction. Not many sixteen-year-olds could do such a thing, but I was good at it. With my social nature, it came easy to me. I excelled at interacting and building relationships with people. From this point forward my career goals were business and entrepreneurship.

On one of the first days of school in grade twelve, I saw Sara for the first time. She was two years younger and new to Oak Park High School. I waved at her from across the hall and whispered to my buddy that I had to meet that girl. I rejoined the cross-country team I had left the year before just to get to know her. Sara and I went out for our first date on her fifteenth birthday, September 16, 1989. We've been together ever since.

My high school yearbook caption reads: "Ambition: Hair at 40. Probable fate: Bald by grad." I pulled my hair loss off in style. I returned to my senior class from a Caribbean cruise in the winter of 1990 with a full beard, a dark tan, and a nearly bald head. I modelled tuxedos for graduation and participated in a variety of school shows. I was always successful at attracting the attention of my peers and teachers.

I went into university knowing business was my path from those early book-selling days. After my first year, I started painting for a company called College Pro Painters and by the next summer had started my own painting company with my best friend, Sandy. We called our company Brush Cuts and it was very successful for a few years. Eventually, I was led to a "real world" job at Bison Transport. It was an unlikely fit for me; transportation wasn't at the top of my list, but the people I worked with were at the core of my decision to pursue a career at Bison. The Bison group grew to be a second family for everyone involved.

Besides working, being active, and interacting with people, travel was a constant factor in my life. I travelled to Europe as a kid for soccer and joined my parents on numerous cruises. On every cruise ship, I managed to get into the inner circle of the crew. Go figure. Immediately after college I took a month off and toured Amsterdam, London, and Wales. Travelling has given me a deep appreciation for good food and fine wine and spending quality time with my loved ones. I cherish these things greatly.

I am passionate about everything I've done in my life. Sara jokes that I have two switches: on or off. If I'm on, I'm fully invested in being the best at whatever I'm currently into. I love making sausages, cooking meat in my smoker, drinking wine, and living *la dolce vita* ("the good life"). I always invest myself in relationships, so I don't have acquaintances; if we are friends, you're immediately in my inner circle. I value loyalty and I'm always ready to help a friend, at any time and in any way. I pride myself on being generous with my time and money.

When Sara and I learned after many unsuccessful IVF (in vitro fertilization) attempts that we would not be parents, I promised that I would be the best uncle ever. Having biological kids wasn't what mattered; what mattered to us was being together. While I'm also not biologically an uncle, there are numerous children who call me "Uncle Darren." I've always been the uncle who provides my friends' kids with new experiences, whether waterskiing, fishing, or shooting guns (to name just a few). I love sharing my toys with the people around me and making a profound impact by teaching them new things and getting them over their fears.

That brings us to the moment when my life changed. It was January of 2011. Sara and I had escaped the freezing Winnipeg winter for a week of sun, sand, and scuba diving in Cancun, Mexico. If you haven't been to Canada in the wintertime, let me explain the cold to you…we're talking bone-chilling temperatures that will leave your skin with burns, called frostbite, if you aren't covering every inch of your face as you walk outside to your car. It's hard to breathe and even harder to move. We were very excited for our little getaway.

Sara and I aren't really into the whole cruise ship, all-inclusive-type vacations. We would much rather explore and create our own agenda. For some reason, though, we had decided we'd take the Club Med route this time and see how it went. It was surprisingly wonderful. There were many packages offered, including snorkeling, scuba diving, trapeze, waterskiing, and windsurfing, so we took on as many activities as we could and enjoyed our time together.

Sara and I have always been adventurous. She's the only girl I know who comes on winter hunting trips with the guys and holds her own. At five-foot-two, she's a badass in disguise and has had my heart since we were teenagers. I always knew I would make her my wife but I never imagined our lives turning out the way they have.

After a few days soaking in the Mexico sun, I woke up with an intense pain in my lower abdomen. I had no idea what it could be; I assumed that the food was disagreeing with me. I decided that I'd continue our trip and hope whatever was going on inside of me would work itself out. I'd never had any serious health problems before, so I figured I had no reason to worry. We continued the rest of our vacation with a little adjustment to deal with the pain and eventually day seven rolled around and we headed home. That morning the pain was absolutely unbearable and I knew I needed to be checked out before flying.

Since it's dangerous to fly when your intestines are clogged up—you could actually burst midair because of the pressure—Club Med hired a doctor, who arrived on a scooter within the hour. He came to our hotel room and listened for sounds in my stomach to be sure my insides were still functioning properly. I was diagnosed with a case of constipation and given the all-clear to fly home.

After a long day of travelling, Sara and I were relieved to be in the comfort of our own home to rest and recover. You know how travelling sick can sometimes make things seem worse than they are? That wasn't the case.

I woke up on Monday still in pain and starting to second-guess the Club Med doctor's diagnosis. I got a second opinion from my local doctor, who agreed that it was a bad case of constipation. He suggested I try over-the-counter laxatives and sent me home hopeful. Nothing worked. I found myself back in his office the very next day with a prescription for industrial-strength laxatives. I thought I must have eaten something *really* funky in Mexico and vowed to be more careful on our next trip abroad.

After two days I still couldn't go to work. I loved my job and my coworkers were amazing people. We all loved working together and had become a family over the years, so when I skipped work yet another day it was clear something serious was going on. By mid-day, I packed up my bags, grabbed a book and my iPad, and drove myself to the Grace Hospital emergency room, wincing in pain and dreading the upcoming wait. In Canada, our emergency rooms are horrible; it takes six to twelve hours before you get any real attention unless your life is threatened. There's a hierarchy queue for care and because I was suffering from constipation, I knew that I would be put towards the bottom of the list.

Sara, the angel that she is, came to the ER on her way home from work to sit with me for a few hours in the hallway. We killed some time together and with no sign of help I eventually sent her home. The next day was her last full day at the office before she headed off to Europe for a work trip. Eventually, around 2:00 a.m., I was seen and given pain medication. They put me on a stretcher in the hallway and told me to get some sleep until a doctor could see me. Sleeping was nearly impossible with "hallway medicine" but at this point I was exhausted from being in pain for more than a week and eventually crashed out for a few hours.

The next morning, I called Sara at the office to give her an update.

"They're going to do a CT scan on me to figure out what's wrong. I'm going to be here for a while longer, but don't worry about it. Keep your flight to Europe and I'll just drive home when they let me out of here." I wasn't really sure what a CT (computer tomography) scan was, but I wasn't too worried and it seemed to go well. That afternoon, a surgeon came over to my stretcher to speak with me.

"We have to perform emergency surgery on you, Mr. Cosentino. We're going to operate either tonight or tomorrow morning," he said.

"Pardon? What do you mean, emergency surgery?" I asked, very confused.

"Well, you've got a blockage inside your bowel; at some point, it will break. We can't have that. If your bowel breaks you become septic and start discharging into your body, poisoning yourself from your bowel. So, yeah, emergency surgery. If not tonight, we'll do it tomorrow morning," he said.

"Okay. Well, what's the cause of it?" I asked.

"Oh, it's probably not that big of a deal. Likely, it's what they call diverticulosis." Seeing my confused expression, the doctor continued. "It's just when you get food stuck that doesn't go through your bowel system and causes inflammation. It's very common but if you don't catch it soon enough it requires an operation to cut the infected area out."

By this point, it was Friday afternoon and Sara was supposed to leave for Ireland the next morning. The last thing I wanted was for her to miss her business trip over what looked like a minor surgery, so I called her to explain the unfortunate news.

"Hey Sara," I said calmly, "here's the deal. I'm going to need surgery. You still go to Ireland tomorrow. The surgeon said it's very common and they just need to get the blockage out before it bursts."

"Darren, I'm coming there. I'm coming there now," she said.

As much as I didn't want my wife to miss her trip, I knew there was no dissuading her when she'd made a decision, so I asked her to stop at Bison to get my laptop. If I really needed surgery, I was going to be there awhile and needed something to keep myself busy. I can't stand being cooped up and bored.

After more discussion with the surgeon and doctor, the common diagnosis was diverticulosis, which is not a disease. If it wasn't that, there were a few diseases that it *could* be. It could be Crohn's, it could be colitis, or it could be cancer. Given the fact that I was thirty-seven years old, active, fit, healthy, with no family history of cancer, that was out of the picture in our minds. Unfortunately, however, there was no way to avoid cutting me open.

The doctor said to me, "The risk factors are pretty low for this surgery. You could develop an infection. There's always a chance in any surgery that it could cause death but those statistics are super low. The one problem we're facing is that we won't know if we'll be able to reattach the intestines until we open you up. We may have to install a colostomy bag, depending on where the blockage is."

At this point, I was terrified.

"We can't have that. I don't want to go through that at all," I pleaded.

"Well, of course we don't want to do that. If you do get one, it just allows your intestines to heal. Then, two months later, we'll open you back up again and reattach your intestines, removing the bag," the surgeon said, attempting—but failing—to comfort me.

All too suddenly, Sara and I realized the surgery I was about to have was a big deal—a really big deal—and that we needed help.

I've always been a caregiver of sorts. I'm the guy people lean on in times of need, whether as a mentor to my godchildren or the work colleague who gets the call to help change a flat tire. My parents were nearly forty when I was born so I began taking care of them earlier than most. Having this surgery was a complete role reversal.

My best friend growing up, Scott Warren, and his sister, Shauna, are the closest people I have had to siblings. When Scott passed away in 1992 after a car accident, I took on the role of Shauna's big brother. For seemingly the first time in my life, I was the one who needed supporting.

The day of my surgery, Shauna happened to be at the same hospital as us, for a routine test. Shauna is a truly amazing human being whom I love deeply. She's strong, independent, and hilarious. She has two little boys whom I love like nephews and her husband works at Bison with me. Sara and I have always spent as much time with Shauna and her family as possible. Through the Bison grapevine, she had heard that I was at the Grace and she stopped by my room after her appointment. We had a nice little chat, joking around in our typical fashion. I was cheered up by her presence and forgot for an instant that I was lying in a hospital bed being prepped for surgery. Eventually, though, we got to the point and discussed the elephant in the room—me.

"So what's wrong with ya, Darren?" she asked, as casually as possible.

"I don't know, Shauna. They think I have diverticulosis. It's this blockage in my intestines from a piece of food that got infected and they need to cut it out before it ruptures and poisons me," I explained.

"Are they sure it's diverticulosis?" she asked.

"Well, it could be Crohn's. Could be cancer." I looked at her and laughed a little. "I don't get fuckin' cancer, Shauna. So it's not that, right? It'll be diverticulosis."

Shauna, who has known me for most of her life, laughed and agreed that there was no way in hell I had cancer. I was too young, too healthy—I was too *everything* to get cancer. Everyone I'd spoken to up to this point was convinced that cancer was mostly out of the question. *Mostly.*

I want to explain something here. We weren't so naïve as to assume that cancer had been ruled out completely. I know that all types of people develop cancer. We weren't automatically dismissing the notion, thinking that only people who are unhealthy get cancer. But with colon cancer there are usually some warning signs: bleeding, abdominal pain, exhaustion, and loss of appetite. With me, everything happened so suddenly. I had pain and before I knew it I was in the emergency room headed into a semi-serious operation.

This being my first surgery, I lucked out. The actual operation was quick and I was back in my hospital room within an hour. In my opinion, the operation was harder for Sara than it was for me (although she would never agree with that).

I woke up from surgery with nurses, lights, and machines surrounding me. I have a pretty high pain threshold but the hours after the operation were worse than I had imagined they would be. People were poking, prodding, and pulling at me. There were needles attached seemingly everywhere for various reasons. The recovery room was not a fun place to hang out, that's for sure. In all of the commotion I looked up at a nurse and asked the only four words on my mind: "Bag or no bag?" The nurse looked at me with a confused expression, processing what I had just asked for a few seconds before telling me that I did not have a colostomy bag.

"WIN!" I thought in my drugged state. I was as ecstatic as you can be coming down from an epidural. I wouldn't have to deal with a colostomy bag! This was a *major* win in our book. Everything was great. And then I lifted up my gown and noticed the forty staples holding me together, immediately bringing me back to reality. I had just been cut completely wide open, skin stretched, intestines severed and reattached. Just a couple of hours ago, there had been hands digging around inside me. Medical thread and staples were all I had keeping my abdomen intact. My feelings of relief started to fade quickly as the pain and harsh reality took over. I didn't know how the nurses expected me to walk the very same day.

A vivid memory from that surgery I hold close to my heart was an overwhelming sense of gratitude and love for Sara. My eyes well up every time I think about that feeling and I get choked up when I try to express it. I remember looking over at her just a few hours out of surgery as she slept in the crappy hospital chair across the room. She had been right by my side all night even after I had told her to go to Europe. Sara kept me strong and distracted as she remained completely calm through the entire process. As she slept in that chair I could see how drained and exhausted she was on the inside, but when she was awake she would never let me know it. I've always loved my wife but seeing her in the hospital room that day gave me an overpowering sense of love and gratitude I can't put into words. It was like I had fallen completely in love with her all over again. I felt the same puppy-dog love you feel when you first meet the person of your dreams. It had been more than twenty years since I first experienced that feeling with Sara. Having it all over again was an unexpected escape from my situation, if only for a few moments.

Eventually, a nurse named Andre broke my little love spell.

"Okay sir, you need to get up. You're going to take two steps today!" Andre spoke with a proper European accent that belied his burly appearance.

"What is this guy talking about?" I thought. "He must have the wrong patient."

"I just got out of surgery four hours ago," I protested.

"Yes, I know; it's time! We want you walking around." Andre wouldn't let up. He helped me up and started to move my legs. I was still pretty out of it from the trauma my body had gone through. Andre scooted me to the edge of the bed and guided me to stand up and sit myself down again. He explained that we'd be walking a bit more each day until I received approval for release.

Overall, my time at the Grace wasn't that bad and I don't have many negative thoughts on the experience. The staff was amazing. There was, however, an obnoxious patient I could have done without. She suffered from dementia, which caused her to call for her caregiver constantly. I had a front-row seat to the show, as her room was adjacent to mine. "Enaaaa. Enaaaa. Enaaaa!" I listened to her sing the nurse's name repeatedly, all day. And all night. "Ena" was the soundtrack to my healing process. After two days I couldn't take it any longer and I got as far away as possible by walking laps around the hospital, determined to get the hell out of there. I desperately wanted to recover in the peace of my own home.

I hate being bored. I can't sit still. I go insane when I can't get up and move. Even though I was still in pain, I was up walking around all day with my IV pole, making it clear that I was gung ho about getting out of the hospital.

On the third night my pain medication wore off and I was sore to the point that I couldn't sleep. It was 2:00 a.m. I hit the call button to get the nurse's attention. When I noticed nobody was coming to help, I looked up to find that the emergency call cord had come off. I couldn't get the nurse's attention because the cord wasn't plugged in. I tried yelling but I was at the end of the hall and couldn't be heard from the nurse's desk. I was getting *really* frustrated. Eventually, I realized that I had my Blackberry with me. I called directory service and got the number to the Grace Hospital. I asked them to put me through to the nursing desk on my floor.

"Nurse's station, Grace Hospital," a voice answered.

"Yeah, is this station thirteen?" I asked, annoyed.

"Yes, this is station thirteen," the nurse said.

"Hi. I'm in bed 221. I'm dying of pain here right now. Can you come?"

"Well, what do you mean you're in bed 221?" she asked.

"I'm a patient, right down the hallway from you. My call button isn't working. Come and see me *please*," I begged.

"But you're calling me?" The nurse was confused. I was desperate for her to hang up the damn phone and come give me some meds. I was also extremely pissed off. Eventually she came to my room and dispensed my medication and the pain subsided. I was resourceful, particularly when the pain meds wore off!

Our doctor had seen my progress and knew how badly I wanted to leave, so he was a little aggressive with getting me out of there. Although it seemed too soon, even to me, he took my staples out before I was discharged. If you haven't had staples removed, let me tell you that it's not fun. Imagine being aggressively pinched in forty places where you've just been cut open and re-sewn.

When I was finally discharged, I was done with hospitals. I never wanted to go back and was so relieved to have this diverticulosis scare over with.

My recovery didn't go as smoothly as my surgery had. It was impossible to walk up and down stairs, so I knew right away that I was sleeping on the couch. No big deal. I spent a week and a half on the couch managing my pain with Tylenol 3s. I was watching TV on a Saturday when I noticed that my shirt was soaked dark red. Bleeding after surgery is common but I'm talking about an abnormal amount of blood seeping through *two* layers of bandages. I'm no doctor but it was clear to me that something wasn't right. I lifted up my shirt and found that my incision had completely broken open in two different spots. I was still healing and extremely sore, so I couldn't get a good look at what was going on. I called Sara to my rescue.

"Sara, this doesn't look good. I'm literally peeling open right now," I said.

Sara took a look. "You know, it's not really that bad, honey. I think I can probably just run out and get some more of those steri-strips and whatever else…" Her voice trailed off. She tried to remain calm but her face was in complete panic. I knew that I was in trouble.

The last thing I wanted to do was head back to the Grace ER, given the wait times. Luckily, the mother of our good friend Tara Hake, Judy, was a nurse and lived nearby. We gave Judy a call and she was at our house in no time to take a look, eager to help. I was disappointed, but not shocked, when she suggested I make an appointment to be seen by a doctor first thing Monday.

The doctor quickly dismissed my belief that I was breaking in half. "This is normal," he said, "Your wound will split open and then you'll heal from the inside out. You may heal with dents in your stomach because of this process but it isn't a big deal. I'm going to take a zinc stick to the places where you've broken open and that should help dry out the wound to speed up the healing process."

"Alright," I thought, "that doesn't sound too bad." The next thing I knew, a giant skewer-like instrument was being poked around inside me. It was going in about two inches and moving around, covering the tissue between my muscle wall and skin. It was not pleasant, that's for sure. The doctor explained some extra wound care to Sara and sent us on our way.

Sara, who previously had no knowledge of my insides, became a pro at taking care of the wound. She must have a stomach of steel because the process is gruesome. She had to take sterile gauze and stuff it in both of the holes now in my stomach before covering them with bandages. It's not a pretty sight, but it's necessary to prevent the surface from healing before the inside does, as that could breed infection.

After an interesting few weeks at home, Sara and I spent our Valentine's Day at the doctor's office. We were beyond ready to put the previous few weeks behind us and get back to our regular lives. As we sat in the waiting room, I distinctly remember this guy sitting across from us looking terrified.

He had a pamphlet in his hand titled *What to Do When You're Diagnosed with Colon Cancer*. Sara and I exchanged glances and I muttered, "Wow, that's the last thing I want to have. We're definitely not going to get that. For sure." We were both feeling pretty thankful that I had got off as easily as I had and the pain of my extra wound care was quickly forgotten. Until we met with the doctor.

"I'm really sorry to tell you, you've got colon cancer. We did pathology tests. We cut out the cancer that was in your colon, but it's moved to your liver. The shadows on your liver that we had originally thought were infection, they're tumours," the doctor explained, morbidly. I could tell the guy was actually really sorry to be telling me this.

The blockage that we thought was likely diverticulosis was actually a large cancerous tumour that perforated my bowel, causing an infection in my abdomen. The doctor explained to us that pathology tests are when they test the tumour itself, before testing a whole selection of lymph nodes. Three out of my twenty-one lymph nodes had cancer.

There are a few moments that are inexplicably awful in my story. This was one of them. Getting a diagnosis of colon cancer was the last thing I had expected, not to mention completely and utterly terrifying. At the time, I was very unfamiliar with cancer. The only knowledge I had of the disease was Sara's mom beating Stage 1 breast cancer and what I had read in Lance Armstrong's autobiography (*It's Not About the Bike*). I knew straight away that my journey was going to be shitty and that chemo was going to be horrible, but given my nature, I was under the impression that I could beat it.

I remember sitting in that office and everything seemed to disintegrate around me for a minute. I thought to myself, "Hey, this is going to suck. There's going to be chemo involved and it's going to be a horrible year, but we'll get through this. The doctor must be making it sound a lot worse than it is. I'm going to be okay." Instantly, Sara and I went into problem-solving mode. There was no mourning; we were ready to take this thing on headfirst. It was the only choice we had, in our minds.

The doctor recommended us to an oncologist named Dr. Harris and we were in her office in four days. This was when things started to become real for us. I can tell you I sure as hell never imagined I'd be sitting in a cancer care office with my wife at the age of thirty-seven, not with the lifestyle I lived. We were shit-scared and had a million questions running through our minds, but we sat and waited together in silence. *What is she going to tell us? What is she going to do? How bad is the treatment going to be?*

When we were called into the office, a nurse and a social worker accompanied us. Dr. Harris was very blunt and got straight to the point, which coincided perfectly with Sara's and my attitude.

"Mr. Cosentino, I'm sorry to tell you that you've got Stage 4 colon cancer. It has metastasized to your liver. You're going to be on a chemo regimen every fourteen days. You'll be receiving chemo for three days— one full day in the hospital and two days at home. You will have a pump with you to safely administer the drugs while you're out of the hospital." Dr. Harris went on to explain how to use the pump and the side effects of chemo.

"Dr. Harris, how long will I be on chemo?" I asked, creating a time-line in my head of how soon we could get over the suck and back to our normal lives.

"You'll be on it indefinitely."

"Well, what does indefinitely mean exactly?" I asked.

"Forever. For the rest of your life you'll be on chemo. Every two weeks," Dr. Harris replied.

"Am I going to outlive my dad?" I asked, not fully prepared for the answer.

"I don't know anything about your dad," she said.

"He's seventy-nine years old and in good health," I answered.

"Well, Mr. Cosentino, given the fact that the average life span of a male in Canada is seventy-five years old, and hopefully we can extend your life by a year or two with chemo, yeah, I think you can outlive your dad. Statistically, you should be able to," she said.

The harsh reality that I might not outlive my dad was an unexpected blow. I felt like I'd been punched in the gut. This oncologist had just told me that I needed to be on chemo for the rest of my life and that it would extend my life by a year or two...*hopefully*. What would the quality of my chemo-filled life be like for that year or two?

I learned that I would be given systemic treatment, which meant that the chemo would not cure my essentially incurable Stage 4 cancer. It would keep me alive, but it wouldn't kill enough of the cancer to cure me. The plan was to treat my entire body with chemo and ideally deliver most of the poison to the tumours in my liver—which would shrink or kill them. At the end of our appointment, Dr. Harris recommended me to a surgeon, Dr. Lipschitz, who might be able to operate on my liver. She explained that if a surgeon was able to successfully cut out all of my tumours, there was a slight chance that my cancer could be eradicated through surgery. Eradicated, not cured. This means that there is no evidence of the disease, however, microscopic cells may still remain.

Sara and I held out hope while we waited for our appointment with Dr. Lipschitz. Although I dreaded being cut open again, living the rest of my life with seventy-two hours of poison every fourteen days was not part of my game plan. We had to find another way.

With no idea of what seeing a surgeon even entailed, Sara and I met with Dr. Lipschitz on March 10, 2011. He is a smaller man from South Africa with the most gentle demeanour you can possibly imagine. In my experience, most surgeons seem mechanical in their practice—they explain what's going on, lay out your options, and you're out the door. There's typically no personal conversation. Dr. Lipschitz proved to be the exception. He was extremely empathetic, giving us ample time to discuss and clarify every question we had. It was a breath of fresh air. Together we looked over my scans. As the doctor put it, the right side of my liver was "littered" with cancer and the left side was "sprinkled" with it—not a good situation for me. Once the cancer has spread to both sides of the liver, it is more difficult to successfully remove all of the cancerous masses. Due to the amount of cancer taking over my liver, the procedure I faced was extremely risky and invasive.

To our dismay, Dr. Lipschitz recommended that we stick to chemo to see if we could reduce the size of the tumours. The smaller the tumours, the easier they would be to remove. From a surgical standpoint, it was necessary to have proof that the chemo was actually working to shrink the tumours before we could operate. Chemo and cancer go hand in hand but most people are unaware that chemo doesn't always work; some people have cancer that is unresponsive to chemo. It always makes you sick but it doesn't always shrink tumours. While it was possible to cut a majority of the crap out, microscopic cancer cells would remain in the lymph nodes and blood. If we could get proof that chemotherapy would work on the large tumours, that was a direct line that it should work on the microscopic cells. We booked an appointment for a few months out to review, Dr. Lipschitz wished us the best of luck, and Sara and I were off to begin our chemo regimen.

The shock we felt after the diagnosis was indescribable. We had no control over this colossal change in our lives. We could easily have let our feelings of helplessness take over and continue to ask, "Why us?" We could have returned home and looked up articles online about statistics, life spans, and side effects. It would have been easy to let cancer and sickness take over our lives, but that's just not how Sara and I do things.

One thing we did have control over was our response to the diagnosis and we immediately chose to act. No, I didn't ask for cancer, but I was damn well going to make the best of it. We were going to continue to live our lives and face the disease from a problem-solving point of view. This outlook has been an extremely beneficial and consistent part of our lives. With every new challenge we follow the same steps—selecting the process that best suits our needs, considering our options, and reaching out to resources built on a foundation of deep relationships. We are polite and sincere in our requests and we always exude a winning attitude. I believe this approach is behind our success in having a team of doctors willing to go above and beyond for Sara and me on our journey.

CHAPTER 2
DO IT MY WAY

Darren and Sara Cosentino

"Uncle Darren is just like Chuck Norris. Uncle Darren is even better than Chuck Norris. When Chuck Norris goes to sleep, he looks under his bed for Uncle Darren."

-Owen and Ben Alford-Burt, "nephews"

On March 18, 2011, we headed to the hospital to get a port-a-cath implanted in my body. If you're going to be on chemo for a finite amount of time, a peripherally inserted central catheter (PICC) is inserted into your arm. A PICC is a long needle with a wire on it that goes into a major vein in your arm, threading through your carotid artery and feeding into your heart. They insert the PICC and you go through a typical chemo regimen: six rounds. Between rounds, they replace the PICC with an industrial-strength IV that is wrapped in gauze for protection and must be kept out of water. When you're going to be on chemo indefinitely, like in my case, they use the port-a-cath. The device looks like a little button and uses a catheter to connect the port to the vein. It's plastic with a rubber nib that attaches to a wire going up into the main blood supply. The port-a-cath makes the process of administering chemotherapy easier, as piercing the skin atop the device administers the drugs straight into the main artery. This eliminates the need to repeatedly search for a vein and thread a tube through for each chemotherapy session. It was easier to access a port-a-cath than it was to give blood; it healed instantly, and I was excited to hear I could swim and shower the very next day.

The vascular surgeon who I was recommended to was a talented but arrogant Englishman. Arrogant might not be the most accurate word to describe him, but he was pretty set in his ways. After he explained the process to me, and what the port-a-cath would do, we went into surgery details.

"It will go over your right chest. You'll be awake yet sedated during the procedure; we'll just open you up and implant it right there," he explained.

"Okay, great. Sounds good, but I don't want it on my right side. It needs to go on my left side," I said.

"Well, sir, we put it on the right because it's an easier operation on that side. The vein that we enter is more accessible from the right."

I looked at him. "But can it be put on the left?"

"Well, it can be, but it's more difficult. It requires a longer procedure," he said.

"Well, put it on the left then," I said.

"No, sir," the doctor replied. "We're putting it on the right. Why do you want it on your left?"

"Well," I replied, ready to argue my case, "I hunt. I need to be able to fire a gun. I don't want it on my right shoulder blade or my right chest because that's where the stock of the gun goes. I want you to put it on the left." It sounded simple to me. Just put it on my damn left side and let's be done with it.

"You'll have to stop hunting then. You'll have to stop shooting," the surgeon said. Now he was really pissing me off.

"No. You'll have to figure out a way to put it on my left side," I said. "I'm not changing what I do, sir. I don't know how much time I've got left, but this is not preventing me from hunting. It's a part of our lives and we're going to continue doing that and everything else we did pre-cancer, no matter what."

I wasn't giving in.

Sara and I were learning to cope with my diagnosis and we had decided that cancer wasn't going to stop us from living a normal life. During the eleven days between chemo treatments I was going to continue living exactly as I had pre-cancer, which meant hunting in the fall. Our strategy was solid and there was no way in hell that a cocky surgeon would prevent us from doing what we love because it was easier for his team. No fucking way.

After a heated debate, the surgeon reluctantly agreed to put the device on my left side and—what do you know—the surgery went off without a hitch.

We got a win in this case. Another one in the bag! I've got cancer, but I can still shoot a gun. Little victories like this one reinforced our desire to find alternative treatments that would allow us to live as we normally would.

Throughout my treatments, we challenged our physicians to consider alternatives to the norm. We were surprised by how many of our questions were answered with puzzled stares. It didn't take long for us to realize that our questions had never been asked before. I'm not sure if this was because I'm so much more active than your average colon cancer patient or if it was because of my powerful desire to be as normal as possible. I realized that the thought of making minor adjustments to treatments might never have been considered. I'm sure this guy had never had a patient with Stage 4 cancer dispute the port-a-cath surgery plan in order to shoot a gun. But Sara and I weren't your typical patients. We constantly took control and didn't accept defeat.

When people get diagnosed with a terminal illness like mine, they tend to check out. They start chemo to prolong life and add time but they don't continue living as they did pre-cancer. I believe this is where people go wrong post-diagnosis. I've heard the same thing from friends who have had parents die of cancer. They let the morbidity of the situation get the best of them—literally. We've always said from the beginning that we don't just want to add time to my life; we want to add active time. If that means my time will be shorter, no problem, but I won't let my treatment get in the way of what Sara and I have planned. I strongly recommend that every person facing health problems adopt this mindset. You need to figure out how to continue living—maybe even live a bit more. You just found out your time has been cut dramatically; don't settle. Early on in our process we reached out to a close friend who was a physician. Her advice was simple: doctors want to find solutions and treatments for someone so young and full of life. In her words, "Be persistent but polite with your doctors." Let me repeat: be persistent! Fight for your quality of life.

After the port-a-cath was implanted, I was told I could no longer chop wood or golf because the motions could break the instrument. I was okay with those setbacks but I continued to throw out questions to the nurses concerning what I *could* still do. They looked at me like I was insane when I asked if I could scuba dive but they told me they didn't see why not.

This is just a glimpse of how my mind works. It starts with an idea: "Let's see, I bet that no one else has gone scuba diving after getting a port put in for Stage 4 cancer, so I'm going to be the one who does it." And then I'll follow through with that idea. It was the same with the hunting drama we had before my port-a-cath surgery. It's not that we're crazy fanatics for hunting, but it's something we like to do. At that point, my thought process was, "Okay, I've got a finite amount of time to live now. If I want to hunt, if I want to do an African safari, I'm not going to sit out for medical reasons. So put the damn port on the other side and let's move along with it." In my head, it was as simple as that.

As long as I'm being safe and taking care of myself, it shouldn't be too difficult to make minor adjustments to treatments and surgeries. I might not be devastated if I can't go hunting but I wanted the option. I want to be the one who pushes the envelope and lives the most incredible life possible with cancer. If opportunity presents itself, you're damn right I'm going to take it. The same goes with scuba diving. I've always been into diving and I know that most people think it's crazy to continue to dive, but when you've only got a couple years to live, you want to be able to cross things off your bucket list. I'm committed to making sure that while I'm alive and healthy I'm able to fulfill whatever dreams transpire. I believe you should do the same.

Early in 2016, I convinced (okay, forced) my close friends to get their scuba diving certification. This was no small feat as it was the dead of winter in central Canada. I was determined to share such an awe-inspiring experience with the people I loved. It was not selfish but rather the opposite. I wanted to push others to have the opportunity to enjoy scuba diving, an activity that I've grown to adore. I was pleasantly surprised that this adventure turned out to be the trip of a lifetime. My buddy Sandy Burt was the first to be "all in" with the idea. No surprise there. I coached his boys from the dock at the cottage by saying, "You want to be the first one in and the last one out." I hope his kids apply my advice as they grow up; I know for sure that it resonated with Sandy. Within four weeks of the call for scuba divers, Sandy was dry-suit certified in Vancouver. Several friends from Bison were equally up for the challenge. Rob Penner, Mike Ludwick, Brad Chase, and Shauna Arsenault took indoor pool courses and pushed to be ready in time for an end of February 2016 excursion to Cozumel. While Mike's wife, Kristin, and my good friend Paula Napier decided to skip the diving, they were extremely excited to come along for the ride.

We were all set for this adventure. We rented two houses with on-site dock access for a private dive boat pick-up. In addition to the Vancouver and Winnipeg crews, our friends Trevor Fridfinnson and Geeta Sankappanavar from Calgary jumped at the chance to join us. I was overwhelmed by the commitment that my friends made to join me on such an adventure. It meant the world to me that they'd invested their personal time and resources in an activity that I was so passionate about.

It was an incredibly gratifying experience exploring the ocean at eighty-foot depths with so many of my closest friends, some of whom were first-time divers. Seeing my friends doing what I loved so much gave me more joy than I'd ever felt diving alone. It was beyond rewarding seeing their faces light up as we shared stories of nurse sharks, eagle rays, and sea turtles well into the evening hours. Each night I prepared a slide show using the nearly one thousand underwater pictures we had taken that day. I'm sure that this slide show was boring as hell for Paula and Kristin, who didn't dive, but for the beginners, Sara, and me, it was amazing. Somehow we tallied up seven consecutive days of diving, including a night dive, which made our final count for the trip fifteen dives. Not bad for a bunch of beginners and a guy with a badly scarred and herniated abdomen.

There was something about having that wetsuit on, all geared up for the deep blue, that made cancer an afterthought. I can honestly tell you that cancer wasn't on my mind while I was exploring the ocean depths with my closest friends, repeatedly forming pyramids on the seafloor and constantly goofing around for the camera. It still blows my mind how lucky I am to have people in my life who will put their lives on hold for me. Cancer reminds you often that it's there and trying to kill you; it would be an unbearable burden to carry alone. My main message in stating that is that you shouldn't be fighting for your life on your own; you must share the load with the people closest to you.

This surreal adventure was interrupted briefly by an incident on our last dive. Sure enough, at seventy-five feet, while swimming through the doorframe of a sunken shipwreck, I managed to clip my pinky finger on a sharp piece of metal. In this case, the treatment was a combination of internal and external stitches to keep my finger held together. But hey, both Sara and I handled this in stride. We kept our cool at seventy-five feet, ascending in a controlled fashion complete with a three-minute safety stop. This was quite remarkable considering I was holding my pinky together by pinching it with the forefinger and thumb of my other hand. At a glance it was an oozing hot mess. Yes, adventurous and challenging activities beyond cancer.

* * * * * * * * * *

Let's get back to chemo. After my port-a-cath insertion, I began a pretty shitty chemo regimen. Chemotherapy is the use of chemicals to treat the disease, specifically the cancer cells. When our body's cells are damaged or die, we produce new ones to replace them. This is done in a balanced way. Cancer cells do not act so orderly. Their division and growth is out of control. More and more of them are produced and they start to occupy more and more space, until eventually they push out useful cells.

Chemotherapy interferes with a cancer cell's ability to divide and reproduce. Chemo drugs may be applied into the bloodstream to attack cancer cells throughout the body or they can be delivered directly to specific cancer sites. For me, the chemo is always applied into my bloodstream, attacking my entire body, including the healthy cells.

My cancer is not curable but it's manageable. Colon cancer is one of the worst cancers out there. I don't think many people get the opportunity to do even twelve rounds of chemotherapy before their cancer takes over their bodies or the chemo makes them too sick. You simply don't get that much time. The typical regimen for breast cancer or lymphoma would be in the four-to-six round range. In most chemo treatments, the patient goes into the hospital for three to five hours. With colon cancer, I had to be in the hospital for eight hours before taking a pump home to administer chemo there for another two full days. It's a tough go. I constantly had to check in with myself mentally and force myself to think positively, to keep plowing through the hard stuff. It wasn't easy.

I remember being in the waiting room for my first round of chemotherapy and thinking, "This is probably the most terrifying thing I have ever had to do." The absolute uncertainty of how bad the effects were going to be was terrifying. The health-care team gives you a little bit of warning about nausea and hair loss but you really have no concept of how bad it will get. All I could do was wait and see.

My first day in the chair I looked at Sara and said, "I wonder what the record is. What's the record for the highest number of chemo treatments ever done, that just keeps people alive 'til they can't take it?" I actually asked Dr. Harris this question a little later and she said she knew a patient that had been on the regimen for a few years. A few years: that was the longest time a patient was kept alive by chemo. At that point I made a commitment to myself that I would be the guy who made it four or five years. Whatever the record was, I would figure out a way to beat it. I would be the guy Dr. Harris mentioned next. If I couldn't get surgery, I would suck it up and do more chemo than anyone had done before. How hard could it be?

From: Darren Cosentino
To: Friends and Family
Subject: Cancer Update
Date: March 31, 2011

Thank you for the overwhelming support these last couple of months. The emails and texts extending best wishes, "How's it going?," and "What can we do for you?" have been very uplifting and appreciated. Please continue to send the emails and texts…I love the attention! That being said, I'm feeling a bit guilty that I haven't responded to everyone's individual inquires, so have decided to send a cancer spam to keep everyone updated.

Today was the start of my chemo treatments. Five hours at the Grace Cancer Care Centre, starting around 10:00 a.m., mostly sitting in a recliner listening to an IV pump the chemicals into my port. Thank God for Sara and the iPad. No real side effects to speak of other than the steroids causing a bit of motor-mouth and some weird muscle twitching, which quickly subsided. The pump is plugged in and running smoothly and will stay plugged in until Friday afternoon when I go back to the hospital to have it removed and flushed. It's held in a very fashionable fanny pack, which I prefer to call a "murse" rather than a "man purse." I'm attaching a photo of me wearing the murse, accented with blue jeans and a dark dress shirt…very stylish, if I do say so myself.

It's now 9:20 p.m. and so far there doesn't appear to be any heavy side effects and I'm really hoping the drugs continue to behave.

Sincerely, your cancer-kicking buddy,

Darren/Cos/Turbo Dog/[insert here any other nickname I may have acquired that you know me by]

P.S. I continue to take the steroids for the next two days and they tend to keep me pretty wired, so don't be surprised if I starting calling you at 3:00 in the morning just looking to chat.

Darren Cosentino

My first six rounds of chemo were surprisingly calm. The first day I went into Cancer Care for treatment wasn't bad at all. They give you a robe and you can sit in nice relaxing lounge chairs and they do a great job of trying to make you as comfortable as possible. There are TVs and magazines and you can have visitors sit with you while you get your regimen. You can even order in food if you're hungry and able to keep it down. Sara and I started to think that maybe chemo would be easier than we'd expected; maybe it would only be three days cut out of my life every two weeks and life would continue to go on as usual.

After the sixth round, the chemo really started to poison me and I became very sick, but by looking at me you couldn't tell. I was still keeping up with yoga as often as possible. Somewhere between chemo cycle ten and fifteen (late 2011) the drugs started to really tear my body apart. I got exponentially sicker and my body just couldn't recover fast enough. I couldn't stop throwing up; it was brutal. Every forty-five minutes I'd be dry-heaving for fifteen to twenty minutes at a time. I was literally living in the bathroom with my head down, telling myself I could get through it and doing my best to man up. With my head in the toilet, I was repeating to myself, "No, I got it. I got it. I got it." The stuff coming out of me wasn't even puke at this point. It was disgusting yellow and orange bile that tasted awful and burned my esophagus, nose, and mouth. My body was completely wrecked and I had no idea how I was going to get through it all but I needed to figure it out and fast. I was throwing up so much that I felt like the stomach acid was burning through the inside of my throat. My acid reflux was worse than ever, as the vomit was burning the valves that typically prevent heartburn.

Chemo is a bitch. It works, mind you, and it continued to shrink my tumours, but it's a bitch. After almost five years and *forty-six* rounds, I've gotten to the point where even thinking about chemo makes me sick to my stomach—I'll puke before the drugs hit my system. My advice for anyone going through chemotherapy is to try as many different methods as possible to lessen the nausea. What worked for me one round often didn't the next. Some favourites have been Slurpees and wintergreen mints. I don't know why but something about having a cold Slurpee to drink while I was getting the chemo kept me from vomiting for a few rounds.

I was prescribed anti-nausea pills but I couldn't keep water down long enough for them to take effect. Soon after I'd take them I'd see them again in the toilet. One sip of water and I'd be throwing up in ten minutes and dry-heaving for twenty more after that. When I wonder what hell is like, I imagine it being better than how I was feeling at that moment. I'll admit part of it is mental; you think about throwing up and it instantly happens. Even right now as I write this I can feel myself wanting to throw up because of the mental trigger that has been ingrained in my brain from so much treatment. It was vital to have something to get my mind off the pain and horrendousness of my situation but at that point my typical distractions were all shot. I couldn't speak, so talking was out of the question. I couldn't even stop puking long enough to play video games. The only thing I could focus on was throwing up and getting through to the ten-minute break, where I could barely catch my breath before the process started all over again.

Not knowing what to do, Sara called Sandy, who lives in Vancouver. He has been an incredible friend to me and super-supportive since day one. Sara knew that if anyone could handle me at my absolute worst, it was him. I'll admit, part of me was wondering what the hell Sara was thinking putting me on the phone. I couldn't speak and I wasn't even on the phone for five minutes before I started throwing up everywhere. I set the phone beside the toilet and I knew Sandy could hear me retching but he didn't hang up. He waited until I could get back on the line to ask if I was okay. "Yeah, I'm good, man," I replied, but I was clearly not okay. I'd speak for a few more seconds and the whole scene would start from the beginning, phone back down by the toilet and more hideous sounds coming from my end.

Soon he was back on the phone with Sara and I could sort of hear them scheming. Sandy is a problem-solver, always has been. He sees a situation and comes up with the best solution in an instant. I could only imagine what he was thinking while listening to me cough up my insides from 1,500 miles away, knowing that Sara would only call him if she had no other option. Realizing that not only was I helpless but that my fearless wife was struggling as well, Sandy lived up to his reputation.

I could tell by the glimmer of hope in Sara's eyes that Sandy had come up with a plan, but she wouldn't tell me what it was. When your body is so weak and depleted you're definitely on edge and I was getting more than a little testy with her.

"What the hell is Sandy talking about, Sara?"

"Sandy has an idea. Just try to rest. We'll give this a shot."

"What is he going to do?"

Sara just gave me a look and I knew she didn't want to tell me, which irritated me even more. I was basically living on the floor of our bathroom now, staring up at her as she paced the room waiting for whatever Sandy had in store. I was not having it.

"I want to fucking know; what is he scheming right now?" I demanded.

"He's got a friend. He's going to get you some marijuana delivered to the house. If you can't keep the marijuana pills down, you're just going to have to smoke it," Sara said.

"Are you kidding me? We're going to have some drug dealer show up at our house while I'm not feeling good? He's going to scope the house out and the next thing we know he's going to be breaking in!" I was in full panic mode, but oddly enough the scenario running through my mind wound up being a good distraction from my sickness, if only for a few moments.

Look, I had never done drugs in my life. Sara and I lived a clean lifestyle and we had no interest in smoking weed. Nothing against people who do; it just isn't our thing. Sandy and Sara knew that I would never agree to have a drug dealer show up at our home with marijuana but they were hoping that I was just miserable enough to try an alternative medicine.

When the doorbell rang, I discovered that this sketchy drug dealer was just another good friend of ours, a typical white-collar middle-class guy. He was at our door within an hour with three joints of medical-grade marijuana that he got from a friend who had been prescribed it for multiple sclerosis. He had called her up and said, "Hey, I got this buddy who's dying on chemo right now. Can you spare a couple joints?" Simple as that. I wasn't able to inhale the marijuana because my throat was so raw from the acidic bile I'd been puking, so it didn't do fuck-all, but it did get my mind off it for a while.

There's a joke among my friends and family that I'm the healthiest sick guy around. It's true; there's nobody healthier than me who's as sick as me. When I'm not on chemo I literally never feel bad. The only time I ever feel slightly off is if I don't get a good night of sleep. Sleep is so pivotal in well-being and is too often overlooked. You can eat healthy and exercise all you want but without adequate sleep your body can't perform to the best of its ability. My one gift to myself since I was diagnosed is that I no longer set alarm clocks or force myself to wake up by a certain time. If I can sleep, I'll sleep. I wake up naturally around 7:30 or 8:00 each morning but if I can sleep until 10:00, I sure as hell am going to.

It's so important for me to stay healthy on this journey. The doctors are doing everything possible to keep me alive so I've got to do everything possible to stay well and make their efforts worthwhile. I've changed my eating habits—I went vegetarian for awhile, I tried paleo, I tried low sugar—whatever I could think of to get me healthier and keep my stamina up for this battle. I truly believe most people can't get the surgery they need because they aren't healthy enough to endure the process.

Fighting cancer is a game of endurance and resilience. As long as your body can handle the grueling treatments—being cut open, having your liver cut in half, and being poisoned for multiple rounds of chemo—and you can recover, the doctors will keep you alive. The minute you allow your body to become unhealthy, the number of options to keep you alive is greatly reduced. I can't stress that enough for other people going through treatments. We absolutely owe it to these doctors to do everything in our power to stay healthy, both mentally and physically.

Hot yoga has been a big contributor to my mental clarity and physical well-being. I've been practicing it since 2009 and I always find it brings me back to a clear state of mind. After I was diagnosed, yoga became the one constant in my life. When I first left my job after fifteen years it was difficult to figure out how to keep busy and out of pajamas. Well, yoga was my answer. When a yoga class starts, it starts. You can't go in late; you have to show up at least five minutes early or you miss the class. By creating my schedule around 9:00 a.m. yoga classes, I kept myself accountable and began to structure my life. When I was really healthy, I would go twice a day—once in the morning and again with Sara in the evening. It was another way for me to win at this whole disease. No one else was going six to nine times a week, so it became my deal. I could do that. During my treatments I made little adjustments to how and when I practiced but I continued to attend yoga as much as I could. I couldn't get enough of it.

While hot yoga was my primary workout, it wasn't the only exercise I got. I was always doing something active, whether paddleboarding during the summer, going on walks around the neighbourhood, or doing work around the house. I spent my days moving my body and keeping busy, which had a profound impact on my "I'm Not Sick" mentality. Personally, I feel it's extremely important to find something physical you love to do, from which you reap both mental *and* physical benefits, and stick to it. You have to stick to your schedule even on the hard days and avoid using illness as an excuse. This mindset goes for everything life throws at you, sick or not sick. Stick out the pain, put in the work, treat your body well, and you will be rewarded.

From the very beginning I told Sara I was not going to be pajama-man. I was going to get up and dressed every morning regardless of how sick I was. No one would see me wearing sweatpants in public. Even if it was my two hundredth day of throwing up, two days later I was dressed in khaki pants and a button-up dress shirt tucked in with a belt. I went to chemo dressed like that every single time. I treated cancer like it was my new job—not a very glamorous job, mind you, but my career goal had become staying alive. For me there was a mental aspect to it. Sara's work has a saying: "Dress casual, work casual." For me it was the same with cancer. Dress sick, you are sick.

CHAPTER 3
OVERWHELMING SUPPORT

Darren Cosentino and Sandy Burt

"Though he was younger than me, this is the guy I looked up to. This is the guy you wanted to emulate. He made whatever room he was in the place to be. You just wanted to hang out with him and catch that "thing" he had. Call it charisma, call it what you want, he had it and you wanted it. I will miss him immensely. He had the ability to make you go further than you ever thought, do things you never could, and kick life's ass along the way. I hope God has a boat and a barbecue and a few projects ready to go, otherwise Darren will drive him nuts!"

- Derek Rush, "cousin"

I've always been very black and white with things. I've never been one to get sucked into the emotional aspects of unfortunate realities. Naturally, once I had mentally defined my new career, the day-to-day steps came easily. Each day was the same—I woke up, got dressed, and took care of whatever "Cancer Sucks" shit I had to overcome that day before resuming my life after hours. My nine-to-five had suddenly become a twenty-four-hour job. But once I had clocked out of my office (also known as my cancer duties for the day) I was living life as I normally would, with minor exceptions for chemo and surgeries. This included cooking dinner for my wife, going to yoga, fixing things around the house, doing yard work, and continuing my active social life. This mentality kept Sara and me from getting sucked into depression. Yes, I had very advanced colon cancer, but it was not my whole life. Cancer was just a shitty job that I had to show up for every day in order to survive. Sara and I were fully invested in this mindset. I looked at cancer as a job that I needed to complete.

While this mentality worked well for Sara and me, it was not as easy for our loved ones to understand. I can't imagine the hurt I would feel being told that someone I cared about had been diagnosed with a terminal illness. Sara and I knew it would take time for our friends and family to truly understand and get on board with our strategy. We knew there was no way to avoid each individual's grieving process. Although facing cancer was an unfortunate roadblock in my life, telling my loved ones what was going on was a full-on mountain directly in front of me. One of the most difficult and emotional challenges I faced during this fight was having to tell my friends and family that I was terminally ill. In a perfect world, I would have told everyone face to face, but that wasn't possible due to my involvement in many social circles. It wasn't even realistic to call everyone individually, so I had to resort to sending out a mass e-mail. I had become the guy who shared such awful news with the click of a button and I felt shitty about it. It felt even shittier to have this news to share in the first place.

It's hard for me to describe how I felt during those times. It wasn't that I felt bad for myself—I knew I could deal with the chaos ahead because Sara and I had a game plan. If I'm given a script, you bet your ass I can nail my part but there is no blueprint for how to tell someone you have cancer.

We were forced to go in blind and the uncertainty made us uncomfortable. As uneasy as we felt, we had to face the facts. We were going to inadvertently hurt people no matter how we told them. There was no question about whether a conversation would be difficult for the people involved.

I felt fucking guilty for having cancer. I felt guilty for taking even a second of someone's happiness. Why should they hurt because of something created inside my body? After all of those years of being the caretaker, I was crushed to be the reason my friends were hurting. But as much as it wrecked me, I had no choice. I had to take a leave from work and I owed my clients and coworkers an explanation. As desperately as I wanted my life to stay the same, some changes were simply unavoidable. I needed to keep my head down and plow through everything—the phone calls, the sympathy, the hurt I was going to cause, the chemo, and the world of sickness that cancer brought.

At the time of my diagnosis I had a wonderful career with a great company that cares about its employees' personal and career growth. I had been working for Bison for fifteen years and loved my job. I wanted to continue to work as much as possible but that meant telling up to two hundred people at work alone that I had cancer. It was a gut-wrenching situation. It was easy to tell people I didn't know very well, "Hey, I've got shitty news. I've got cancer. My plan is to keep working as much as I can but once I start chemo I'll be done working in the office." Cancer is so prevalent in the world today that people have become numb to the news unless it directly affects them.

I wish it had all been that simple. I've known some of my Bison coworkers my entire adult life. Some of them I personally brought on as Bison employees. We had become a family. I couldn't get two words out of my mouth before breaking down in front of these people. I couldn't even say, "I've got..." before I'd start bawling in my office.

Admitting I had cancer was, quite honestly, embarrassing. I was ashamed to tell people that I had cancer and ashamed for feeling ashamed. I had never associated shame with a terminal illness; why was I feeling this way? There was nothing that could have prepared me for the emotions that hit me. Sometimes our feelings defy logic. There's no right or wrong way to feel when you're fighting for your life. It was tough at first but I learned to go easy on myself for feeling this way. After all, I had to save that energy for kicking cancer's ass.

As shitty as it was to break the news, things got better because we had so much support. There have been an immeasurable amount of real heart-wrenching moments throughout our journey that have kept Sara and me going on rough days. I was surprised by the people who came out of the woodwork to help. One example was my co-worker, Mike Ludwick. Mike was Sara's childhood neighbour and she had been friends with his wife, Kristin, in high school, but we weren't close friends pre-cancer. When Mike heard that I had cancer, he immediately went into problem-solving mode. It didn't matter that we weren't close; he immediately joined Sara's and my team.

"Okay, you've got cancer. It's shitty but let's make sure we look at all of your options. My sister is a doctor, a pathologist, and I'm going to call her immediately. We're going to get her to give you some direction on where to get second opinions and what those opinions mean from a medical standpoint." Mike shared our mindset and we quickly became incredibly close friends. He gave us so many pep talks in those early days. He used to call us randomly and say things like, "All you've gotta do, man, is just get through the first cycles of chemo. Cancer is changing every single day and they're figuring out new ways to beat this, so just get through the first six months. Don't worry too much about it. Yeah, it's going to be shitty, but suck it up, get through it, and they will figure out a solution for you at the end." We've kept that mentality this whole time. It's what kept us going some days and I'm always replaying that conversation in my head. On bad days and good ones I find myself thinking, "Okay, remember what Mike said. I've just gotta get through this next step. Yes, there is going to be some chemo involved before or after surgery and as much as I'm dreading that, I just need to get through those weeks and months and I'll be okay."

This was not the reaction I expected from a work acquaintance. We were very lucky to receive an outpouring of kindness and direction from Mike and his sister, who also jumped in to help in any way she could. We sent her copies of the CT scans we'd received and got her medical opinion. I had never met this girl and yet she was doing research for us: reading my scans, reading the pathology reports, interpreting, shooting emails to co-workers about our story, and helping us figure out what to do next. She even got in contact with an oncologist she had gone to medical school with for yet another opinion.

Paula Napier is another work colleague who became family. Although our interactions before cancer had been brief, she has become a great friend. She checks in with Sara and me regularly and keeps me up to date on what's happening at Bison. Her dedication to keeping me involved and her availability for last-minute meals, drop-in visits, and rides to chemo treatments have been immeasurable.

I've found that if I focus solely on getting through that first bit, as Mike said, someone is going to come up with a solution that works for me. While Sara and I created this positive thinking plan from the start, I found I had to remind myself daily to focus on the solutions. I had to constantly check in with myself to avoid becoming a victim, which could ruin me. The solution in my case was surgery. Although there was no magic drug to cure colon cancer, doctors were coming up with new ways to treat my disease and new surgical procedures. My first task was to find a surgeon who would cut me open. If that wasn't possible, we would head to Toronto for radiation treatment on my liver.

* * * * * * * * * * *

Throughout my treatments, I've learned so much about supporting loved ones during difficult times. Before cancer, I wouldn't have known that endless calls asking for updates and the best times to visit weren't actually helpful in the healing process. There is a sense of guilt instilled in the patient and the focus becomes comforting the healthy person. I knew I was lucky to have so much support but I often wound up having to fake a smile and pull myself together to make the people around me feel better.

Sara put it best: "Everyone that's been in contact with us wants to help, wants to give empathy, wants to do something. Only a few people have been able to figure out what is really helpful." Don't get me wrong, I appreciated each and every bit of support, but the best support Sara and I have received is when people take the initiative to make things easier on us. The motivating text messages and emails from people letting me know they were thinking of me rather than asking for updates were great, as were the texts that said, "You're strong!" "You can do this!" "Focus on yourselves, you've got this." We've had neighbours we barely spoke to mow our lawn and shovel snow from our driveway without even mentioning it and friends who cooked us meals without being asked. Sandy never called to ask when he could visit; he booked ten flights for random days and if I was in chemo throwing up he'd be sitting right beside me. He knew that just being there was what mattered and because he planned his trips without needing anything from me, they were always stress-free visits.

It's been truly incredible when friends have done things with the sole purpose of making things easier on us. We've had a lot of outstanding, amazing support from our friends. This support has not only helped with everyday life, but with getting more out of life. When we told Sandy that we were making a short escape to Las Vegas for four days between chemo cycles in December 2011, he sprang into action. Sara and I stayed at the Venetian hotel in an awesome three-bedroom, three-bathroom suite that even had a TV in the bathroom. I loved the suite; we had spent good money on it and I was perfectly content to relax there for the night. Sara, who's normally early to bed, insisted that we go out to see Caesar's Palace, so I reluctantly got off my butt and she dragged me out on the town.

As we went down the escalator, Sara turned and started talking to a stranger. I looked at the guy and thought how weird it was that he looked so much like my best friend. I couldn't believe she knew someone in Vegas who looked exactly like him. Of course, it was Sandy. Sara and Sandy had planned an incredible surprise for me. Sandy was only in Vegas for a day and a half and it happened to be his birthday, so of course we went all out. Sandy threw out ideas in his typical fashion: "What do you want to do, Darren? Do you want to go on a roller coaster? Do you want to get a tattoo? Do you want to shoot guns or go gambling?" We literally only had twenty-four hours to explore Vegas together and it was 10:00 p.m. I was just a day and a half off of chemo, yet the party went on.

We went for eighty-dollar servings of Kobe beef, we smoked cigars, we went gambling, and then I mentioned hitting the Stratosphere hotel to ride the rollercoaster. Sandy attempted to shut that one down really quickly.

"Yeah, I'll do any rollercoaster. We're not doing that one."

"What are you talking about?" I asked.

"Well, it's terrifying. I rode it once and I'll never, ever, EVER do it again," he said.

Riding the Stratosphere became a challenge. We had to ride that rollercoaster while we were in Vegas. As we were buying the tickets, Sandy bet I was the only guy that had gone through two intense surgeries and just finished his twelfth round of chemo days ago that had ridden that rollercoaster. I needed to add it to my growing list of things I'd done that "sick" people don't do.

The ride started out pretty uneventfully. We were hanging over the edge of the building but it was no big deal. Suddenly the whole train of cars sped up to about fifty miles an hour before coming to a complete stop. This repeated multiple times before the ride dropped forty-five degrees and we were facing the ground. The Stratosphere is crazy high. The only thing that held me in my seat was a lap bar that repeatedly reminded me of the recent trauma to my abdomen and that I had been throwing up just days before. I was in the very front of the car and I thought I would fall out. And if I didn't, I would die from popping open. I had already been cut open both directions on my stomach and I had a sudden fear there that the rollercoaster would be the end of me. When we made it off, I felt a huge rush from conquering something most sick people would never do. It was a crazy experience made incredibly special by Sandy's company. Just another example of the truly amazing things my friends do for me.

At the beginning of my fight with this disease, Mike, Kristin, and Paula started a tradition of having Sara and me over for weekly dinners. No matter how rough I was feeling, I got a good night's sleep the night before, made sure I was shaved and showered, and forced myself to feel good. We would pretend I didn't have cancer that day so there was no being sick or feeling sorry for myself. When we went to their house everything was normal again. I always looked forward to those dinners.

Mike Ludwick, Kristin Ludwick,
Darren Cosentino and Paula Napier.

Another remarkable example of unwavering support is my ninety-year-old Auntie Virgie. She often supplied her infamous "hello dollies" (scrumptious dainties), soups, pasta sauces, and other random foods for us. Virgie showed that she is thinking of us and doing what she can by making these goodies. She was not looking for praise or for thanks and she was so sincere in her love for us.

We have a similarly kind couple at our lake home, Gord and Lynne McCoy. On a number of occasions, we arrived at our cottage to find a bag filled with special treats for us to share with our guests. No strings attached!

These people are guided by an internal inspiration to commit unconditional acts of kindness. Following every single surgery, our friends Lisa and Mike Krak reached out to their network of friends to supply weeks' worth of meals for us right to our door. Friends and family always took the initiative to make us feel loved as they helped with our everyday needs. These deeds would be the closest thing I can relate to acts of God. Perhaps there is some higher power that influences the timing of these actions.

Sara Cosentino, Sandy Burt, Ben Alford-Burt,
Owen Alford-Burt, Darren Cosentino.

Sara and I love to host friends at our beautiful cottage near Lake of
the Woods in Kenora, Ontario, about two hours from Winnipeg. We've
owned it for ten years and it's a beautiful, homey little spot right on
the water with a boathouse and a private dock. The Winnipeg River is
completely surrounded by a beautiful green forest and the water is full of
walleye, northern pike, perch, and bass. The fishing is amazing. When the
weather is nice I'm also happy to spend hours in the boat with my line in
the water without catching a thing. We own paddleboards, a kayak, and
boats, and love nothing more than filling our little slice of heaven with the
people most important to us while we drink wine and cook meals to share.

We still spend a lot of time at the cottage but once I got sick, hosting
became a little harder. I'm very independent; I don't like to burden people
and I don't want guests feeling like they need to dote on me just because
I'm sick. I want them to get out of the house and reap all the benefits the
beautiful lake has to offer. Five years ago, we wouldn't have cared how our
guests spent their time or if we wasted a weekend of nice weather on an
unadventurous visitor. Before cancer, Sara and I weren't so extreme about
houseguests but with limited time left we simply have to make the best
of every single hour. We can't have someone coming to dote on us and
remind us that, yeah, I have fuckin' cancer. We want guests that are up for
the ride. If I've gone through as many rounds of chemo and surgeries as I

have, you'd better be keeping up with me. If someone jumped in the lake or got on a paddleboard and kept up with me, or at least tried to, they would be invited back repeatedly.

Not only are we particular about only wanting guests who partake in what the lake has to offer, we also surround ourselves with people who make us laugh. The guys at work found out that I had had surgery and some of them came to visit. We'd always been real tough guys at work. Nothing could put us down so an operation definitely wasn't going to. I was in the hospital for seven days recovering but still using my Blackberry to email and call clients from my hospital bed. It was essentially all business as usual, except for the fact that I had just had a large chunk of my intestine removed. I was making lots of calls and even more jokes than usual and things were going really well.

People from work sent a collage over to the hospital as a get-well present. It was full of pictures of Shauna's husband, Paul, and they were pretending to promote him to my position! The poster had pictures of the vice president of Bison handing off my office to Paul with a giant grin on his face. There were pictures of Paul sitting in my chair with his feet up on my desk right next to pictures of Sara. The card read, "Hey, you've been gone for three days so we've taken over your spot. We found a replacement for you." They got everyone in the office to sign the card for me. It was very nice that everyone pitched in and made a joke of the whole situation because that continued to be our defense throughout this whole thing. In response, Sara sent a picture of me flipping them off, saying, "Fuck you guys!" Practical, funny shit, done without prompting: that's what helped me heal in the hospital, not tears and deep conversation.

Bison Transport has been a remarkable support system for me since day one. Peter Jessiman, the owner, and Rob Penner, the president, are two of my greatest friends and they've done so much for Sara and me. Peter is the one who pushed me to write this book. If not for him, this book would not have been written and my story would be forever limited to the group of people who touched my life. Rob has been an incredible source of laughter and adventure. He has hosted us at his lake home in Muskoka and visits our cottage to drink beer and fish as often as his schedule allows. I am beyond grateful to have worked for such an amazing company, one that truly cares about its employees. I wish I could give back what I have received.

We have been so lucky to have friends and family that drop everything to support us. These friends have opened their homes to us when we were in their towns for treatments, accommodated our eating habits, given us space, and let us use their homes as our own. They've gone above and beyond and we couldn't be more thankful. Norm and Maryann Sneyd have hosted us in Toronto on a number of treatment trips. They welcome us without hesitation and cater to our every need. These treatment trips are scary and emotional but having Norm and Maryann as our guardians away from home has been incredible. This couple is an inspiration to all who know them and two of the most generous and thoughtful friends we have.

Sara's mom, Mary Koonz, handles the nursing duties during Sara's work hours. Mary and I get along very well. She is truly a caregiver with a single agenda—to help us with our journey. No expectation of praise or payback, just pure parental love and support. Mary is always available in a heartbeat despite living eight hundred miles away in Shawano, Wisconsin.

My parents' reaction was another story. I'm hesitant to write about them, but since I vowed to tell every part of my journey they have to be included. My parents, Ramon and Doreen Cosentino, are very loving and have the best intentions, but as their only child, I feel immensely guilty about my disease. I love them to pieces, yet I refused to have them up to the cottage. Because of where we live, there is such a short time that Sara and I can enjoy warm weather and outdoor activities. Between June and October, we spend as much time as possible at our cottage. My parents are so caught up in their own lives and health problems that I don't believe they truly realize how sick I am. When they visit, it's all about them— how badly their knees hurt, how they can't sleep, how I don't take them fishing enough. The list is never-ending. I do have to take some of the blame for giving them this sense of security around my life and well-being, though. I'm more active than they have ever been in their lives. How could I be sick?

What I'm getting at here is that with a terminal diagnosis, I had to be selfish. I had to put myself—my needs, wants, and desires—before the people who could not support my vision. I couldn't allow guilt to keep me from living my final years in pure happiness. I wish it was that easy for everyone and that it didn't take cancer for me to spend every day exactly as I pleased, but I'm grateful for the ability to stay positive and inspire others to do the same. I want you to know that you control your life. Don't wait to be diagnosed with Stage 4 colon cancer to cut the negative people out of your life and truly embrace your passions.

It's painful to think about what my parents will do once I'm no longer physically here. I know Sara will take care of them and help them through the process but it's very distressing to picture them outliving their son. From the first diagnosis all I wanted was to outlive my father and I've striven for that goal ever since. If I do die before my parents, I want them to know that I lived the last years of my life the happiest I had ever been. I hope that they read this book and know that I was blessed with an amazing, incredible life full of adventure, kindness, and love. I want them to know that I love them immensely and that they've been wonderful parents. They've always done their best. I can't even fathom being put in their shoes.

Another incredible support system Sara and I have had on our sides is our medical team. My gratitude for physicians and treatment teams is infinite. I am so humbled by their abilities, personal investment in the medical field, and drive to keep me alive. We've been very lucky to work with such incredible, supportive doctors and surgeons who go above and beyond every single time. There were a number of interactions with nurses and physicians that helped us endure challenging hospital stays. My memories of physical pain and mental anguish are overshadowed by their helpful words of encouragement and the special accommodations and extra attention they so graciously gave us. There are so many incredible people doing extraordinary things in health care and I am thankful for every one of them. Not a surgery or hospital stay went by without Sara delivering personal thank-you notes accompanied by Starbucks coffee boxes and sweets. I am constantly seeking to personalize my expressions of appreciation. There is really no way to truly reflect my gratitude, but that has never stopped me from trying. For any health care workers reading this, please know the profound impact you have on cancer patients. Whether it is the positive outlook you bring to a shitty situation (both literally and figuratively) or the extra time you take to explain how procedures work, God bless all of you.

There are a number of close friends who have stayed with us in this fight, every step of the way. Five years is a long time. Think about how your social circles change in the period of completing a secondary and perhaps graduate degree. They can change a lot. Not this group. The timing of their check-in calls, e-mails, and offerings of their homes continued to be a regular boost for me. Both Sara and I have been so blessed by such remarkable support throughout this journey.

CHAPTER 4
TRUE GRIT

Darren Cosentino

"In our eyes, Darren single-handedly redefined what it means to be tough. Not only did he fight with epic determination, he did so with class and humility. He was kind, generous, funny, and eternally optimistic for himself and everyone around him, even as he battled daunting odds. It was an honour to work alongside him and he is someone who Dana and I will never ever forget. In life, we can only hope and pray that we will be able to positively influence the lives of a few. Darren left an indelible and immensely positive mark on the lives of many."

-Peter and Dana Jessiman, friends

When I was diagnosed, I was very lucky that the doctors were able to successfully cut the infected part of my intestine out so that I could eat and use the bathroom normally. The problem was with my liver, where the cancer had spread; I had tumours all over my liver that needed to be shrunk with chemo, cut out, and shrunk again. Luckily, the liver is an amazing organ that can rebuild itself up to sixty percent. I just had to find a surgeon that would do the operation. While Sara and I waited to see if Dr. Lipschitz would be willing to do the surgery, we researched and got in contact with other surgeons all over Canada and the U.S. so that we would be ready with a backup plan if he denied the surgery. We had CT scans lined up to send to every surgeon on our list across North America to prove that my tumours were responsive to chemo, which is one of the deciding factors in determining whether to do surgery.

One of the frustrating things about the Canadian health care system is that everything takes a lot longer to get done than you think it should. When you get cancer, you're generally expedited and you get your scans back promptly but it's still slower than that in the U.S. In Canada, an oncologist has to send a reference letter to a surgeon, who may need to consult with a radiologist before you will hear back. Because U.S. health care is a paid service and more of a business than in Canada, things seem to go at a swifter pace. It simply takes longer to get an answer for anything in Canada than in the U.S.

By taking the fastest course of action, we wound up in New York at a beautiful hospital, Sloan Kettering, for a pre-op appointment with a surgeon who was willing to do the procedure. I had just gotten off chemo so I was sick as a dog. I wasn't throwing up but I was as close as could be and feeling miserable. We met with a nurse, an oncologist, and a surgeon: arguably the best oncologist in the U.S. and probably one of the top three liver surgeons. It was a quick and easy decision for them—they would do the liver resection.

Because the procedure is extremely invasive, it was important that my body be as strong as possible. The liver surgeon recommended I get off chemo for four to six weeks before the operation. I needed to build my immune system back up before he could cut the right side of my liver out and use radiofrequency ablation (RFA) to destroy the tumours on the left side.

RFA is a process that can be done internally or externally. A long needle touches directly on the cancerous tumours. The doctor watches the needle ablate the tumour on an ultrasound screen. Since they would already be cutting out a section of my liver in this procedure, the RFA process would be relatively simple.

In addition to this surgery, we were shooting to get a newly invented puck that a Sloan Kettering oncologist had created implanted. The puck is designed to pump chemotherapy directly into the liver by using atmospheric pressure to squeeze the medicine into the body. It would go inside my abdomen with a tube connecting it to my liver. With this puck plus systemic chemo—the regular type that pumps throughout the entire body—there was a ten to twelve percent higher success rate of eliminating cancer long-term. Things were looking pretty good but I would have to return to New York once a month for monitoring in addition to my two-week routine of chemo.

Although I was feeling positive about the operation, Sara and I weren't sure about the financial side of it. The whole procedure was looking to be between $250,000–$500,000. If New York was our only option, we were committed to finding the money. We would remortgage our home, pull out our retirement savings, and do whatever we had to in order to get this shit cut out of me. If I had to fly to New York every month for a few days of chemo, I would have to relocate there. I didn't want to add unnecessary travel and stress to my life when I knew I'd already be exhausted. Sara and I had started to go through options of how we would move and what we would do for money when we realized that she would have to leave her job. Because she was our only breadwinner, this was not ideal. We knew in our hearts we had to keep searching and pushing for a doctor in Canada to do this procedure. At least we had an option. We were looking for any way out at this point.

With a new plan beginning to form in our minds, Sara and I headed back to Canada feeling a combination of relief and stress. We contacted Dr. Harris to let her and her team know that the operation was possible in New York but that we would much rather stay in Canada. Anywhere in Canada would be better than spending a quarter of a million dollars and having to move to New York. We wanted to speak with Dr. Harris in person immediately to avoid wasting precious time, as we knew the Canadian health care system would take a while. Within a few days, she called us back. At first we were a little nervous that she would be upset with us for traveling out of Canada. She had done so much for us and been an incredible oncologist and we didn't want to step on anyone's toes. But she was understanding and always supportive of us seeking out alternative treatment options. She's been the perfect oncologist for us and we're so thankful for her.

"You do what you need to do and I will support you one hundred percent," Dr. Harris said after we explained our trip to New York. "The New York oncologist that you saw called me already, actually. I hear great news that the surgery is a possibility there. I'll start applying to see if the Manitoba government will pay for that surgery for you. If the treatment isn't offered in Canada but is somewhere else in the world, there's a possibility that they will cover it. I'll put you on that path right away. Come see me next week for a consultation. Let's get this ball rolling."

Dr. Harris knew how sick I was getting from the chemo; it was very clear I couldn't keep up with a chemo regimen forever. Sara and I desperately needed this surgery to have a chance. Our health-care team in Manitoba teamed up with the New York physician and things started to go in the right direction. It was liberating to know that the oncologist I saw in New York had taken it upon herself to contact my oncologist in Manitoba before I had even seen her. A sense of relief washed over me when I knew that things were moving behind the scenes. It started to look like we actually might be able to eradicate my cancer with a liver resection.

It amazes me when physicians work together and really put their hearts and souls into creating a solution for patients. My team saw how hard I worked and researched, how well I treated my body, and how badly I needed to find a cure. My enthusiasm and resilience inspired them to fight my battle alongside me.

Dr. Harris is a little firecracker. She's militant, aggressive, and blunt—almost to the point of offending people when she talks. When she's in charge, shit gets done. When she learned at our follow-up appointment that I hadn't heard back from my Winnipeg surgeon, she was not happy. She immediately got on the phone and called him.

This does not happen in Canada.

Doctors write reference letters here and you'll receive a call maybe two weeks afterwards to make an appointment for a few weeks later. Doctors typically don't make personal calls to each other on a patient's behalf. I had some pretty amazing people in my corner and I felt important that day.

"I need to speak with Dr. Lipschitz," Dr. Harris demanded.

"He's doing rounds right now, ma'am. He's unavailable."

"Well, I need his pager number then," Dr. Harris replied.

"We don't normally do that, ma'am. Can I take a message?"

"So you're saying Dr. Lipschitz isn't in the operating room? He should be operating all day. If he's not in the operating room there better be a good reason for it. Give me his cell phone number."

The hospital attendant obliged and soon Dr. Harris was on the phone with Dr. Lipschitz—who happens to be the nicest man ever.

"Okay. I've talked to Mr. Cosentino. He's gotten back from New York. Apparently, they're able to do a surgery. They offer this procedure there. Why can't we do it here in Manitoba? When can you see him?"

Sara and I sat in Dr. Harris' office listening to her side of the phone call and wondering if this type of attack just might work. We were very hopeful, as always, and we felt confident knowing that we had our New York back-up plan. If we had the surgery in Manitoba, it would make a world of difference for us financially and personally. We wanted to live our lives as close to normally as we could, which seemed highly unlikely with a big move to New York on the horizon. Magically, with the help of our bad-ass oncologist, we got a phone call about a cancellation in the surgeon's office and Sara and I headed in to see Dr. Lipschitz a few days later.

Dr. Lipschitz explained to us that his hospital had the same equipment as the New York hospital and that it was possible for him to perform the surgery but that it was very risky. A liver resection has about the same risk as heart surgery. There is an extreme risk of infection and a million little things that could go wrong, leading to liver failure. There was a chance that I could die from the surgery. There was a slight chance of a nick in my bowel, which would poison my body from the inside. But I had no alternative besides chemo, and after researching it thoroughly, Sara and I decided these were risks we were willing to take. This procedure was my best chance at living the rest of my life active and happy. I knew if chemo was the only option I would not want to prolong my life in that miserable, awful state. My body just couldn't take much more poison.

We decided that I would get a liver resection but the puck idea was out. There had been no other hospital at the time with the same results as Sloan Kettering when it came to inserting it. They had tried in Japan and Texas but with nowhere near the same success. The puck would also have limited my abilities activity-wise, as it would have been carried around in my abdomen. Scuba diving would definitely have been out, with the changing atmospheric pressure. If we had the option to cut out sixty percent of my liver, stay in Manitoba, and save $250,000, we would skip the eight percent higher chance of my cancer being eradicated with the puck. If everything went well, the surgery would be another win to add to our growing list.

I think most of the surgeons and doctors we dealt with were surprised at how aggressive we asked them to be. When given bad news, I think most people are unsure whether or not to move forward. I believe that most of them, if given the option, would choose to stay on chemo rather than face the risks that arise with surgery. I tell the doctors point-blank that I would take them killing me on the operating table while fighting a good fight over living my life on chemo. I don't care what the risks are. If there is any chance of bettering my life, I want to be put on that operating table. I will always take that risk. It's all or nothing with Sara and me. I've told my surgeons, "You've either got to cure it or let's get on with the program. Let's move forward with operations and procedures. If there is a way to eradicate the cancer, I'll take whatever risk is involved." This whole process has been about quality of life to me, not quantity. I don't need to live long but I need to live well.

A lot of the success that Sara and I have had has been because of our attitude. I walked into surgery that day; they didn't take me in on a stretcher. I put on my gown and walked into the operating room, saying, "Hey guys, I'm here! Let's cut out my gunky liver!" I acted like it was just another day at home or in the office. We were gung-ho about getting cancer beaten. We were always optimistic, pleasant, and strong instead of worried. Never once did we focus on the fact that this could be the worst thing ever and we haven't shed a single tear about cancer since the day I was diagnosed. I've gotten very emotional and about the support that I have and the friendships I've been blessed with, but never about the cancer. We've just dealt with it. This time, we dealt through surgery.

In asking our doctors to go to extreme lengths, we've always been attentive and showed our appreciation. After my colon resection, I told Sara that a hospital cleanup staff member had been especially sweet to me. The next day, Sara brought in chocolates and a travel pack of Starbucks for the woman. We aim to radiate positivity and we want people to realize the little everyday things they do have a huge impact on us. We've learned to get some enjoyment out of hospital stays by being so appreciative and positive. We have had a lot of fun there together and we both have loads of memories from different hospital stays that make us smile. Life can be really good if you choose to see things from the positive side.

After my twelve-hour surgery (triple what had been scheduled) we got some bad news. The right side of my liver had been cut out successfully but the left side was littered with the disease. There was a lot more cancer than they had anticipated, so the radiofrequency ablation procedure had been abandoned. RFA would have put my liver function in jeopardy, given the amount of cancer there. Although Dr. Lipschitz was calm, we knew he had been completely shocked when he cut me open. He wouldn't have done the surgery if he had known how much the cancer had spread within my liver. I was lucky that he hadn't known. Now we had to find a solution to yet another problem. We knew we could find a way eventually, so we focused on healing and moving forward like we always did—as a team.

From: Sara Cosentino
To: Friends and Family
Subject: Cos - Update 2
Date: August 20, 2011

Hello,

Darren's liver functioning continues to show improvement. He is now eating and we were able to harvest his homegrown tomatoes to satisfy his craving for a tomato sandwich.

He devoured a serving of dim sum I brought him yesterday—an excellent sign. Late yesterday afternoon, Darren negotiated his release from the hospital. It was textbook. The team of surgeons stopped by to see him at 5:00 p.m. They said that things continued to improve and asked how Darren felt about being released tomorrow. His response: "Thank you, that would be really great. It would be even better if it was earlier." The surgeon team collaborated and collectively endorsed a late-day discharge.

Rest assured, Darren left the hospital in fine form. Having not anticipated release that early, his attire consisted of slippers, a full-length boxing robe (without a t-shirt), and fleece pajama pants with black bears on them. Despite him looking like an escapee, we made it.

With this early release, Darren returns to the HSC on Monday as an outpatient. He will need more blood work (as his counts continue to be low), his staples will need to be removed, and his external drain will be reassessed. But for now—freedom! Once he rebuilds his cell counts Darren will be open for visitors. We are hopeful that this will be by early next week.

Your continued support, prayers, and encouragement are appreciated. Thank you!

The next month was exceptionally challenging. With so much trauma to my body, my recovery started with several days in ICU step-down. This was an incredibly noisy room with bells and whistles constantly going off. I struggled to sleep and could barely move with the number of contraptions hooked up to me. There was one night in particular I distinctly remember; the alarms on the machines hooked up to me went off every fifteen minutes. I found this so frustrating; I was craving sleep, deep sleep, knowing that would accelerate my healing. Instead, the alarms were constantly tripped and I was going insane. It wasn't until the next morning that a nurse pointed out the pulse reader attached to my finger. Turns out, I was setting the alarm off each time I moved my finger to my chest while I was trying to sleep. "Good grief," I thought to myself, "that would have been nice to know eight hours ago."

After the bells and whistles of the step-down unit, I spent a few more days on a post-surgery ward. I was always so determined to get out of the hospital. When I knew that Dr. Lipschitz and his entourage were coming for their rounds, I would put my game face on and be ready to dance a jig. I was discharged after seven days and sent home with an external drain dangling from my abdomen. The drain was for collecting bile and fluids that continued to seep from areas of my liver that had not adequately scarred over yet. It was gross, to say the least. Not only was it a dangling extremity, it was full of the discoloured fluids that my body continued discharging. The expectation was that the amount of fluid collecting in the drain would gradually lessen, but that didn't happen. The bile leak continued and three weeks after surgery Dr. Lipschitz made the decision to pull the drain regardless of the continued fluid collection.

In the small observation room at the hospital, I braced myself for the drain extraction. I knew the tube was quite long and connected to my liver via my abdomen but I convinced myself that the pain would be short—like tearing off a Band-Aid. I was not prepared for what happened. Immediately after the drain was pulled I felt an indescribable burning sensation and excruciating pain throughout my abdomen. I curled up on the observation table like a little baby. Dr. Lipschitz suggested that I stay put for a while to see what would happen and injected a fast-acting painkiller into my arm. I rolled around on the table in pain for hours.

Eventually, the call was made to perform an emergency CT scan. Something was clearly not right. Dr. Mottola, the lead radiologist at the Health Science Centre hospital jumped into action and I was wheeled down to have my abdomen checked out. Results from the scan were available immediately; there were no signs that further intervention could be performed at the time. Much to my dismay, the action plan was to go home, rest, and monitor the pain. Sara and I drove home and every bump in the road sent me over the edge—and I have a high pain threshold. Within an hour of arriving home, I could not take the pain any longer. I knocked on the wall of our bedroom to get Sara's attention. She was on a work call but she bounced up the stairs with the phone still in hand. I kindly but sternly requested that she dial 911. An ambulance arrived, sirens blaring, within fifteen minutes. I rode in the ambulance and Sara drove her car behind us. We had no idea how long my stay might be or just what sort of action plan might be in store for me.

It took hours to be seen by an emergency room physician, which meant hours with no pain meds. As soon as I was admitted, they injected me with pain meds to help calm me down a little. Although it was known that I was experiencing a leak in my abdomen, the treatment team didn't have a viable option for clearing things up. They thought that the liver would scar sufficiently to stop the leaky fluid. In the meantime, pain management was the prescription. I was exceptionally thankful for that plan at the time.

Over the course of a couple weeks I had multiple CT scans to check the status of my bile leak. Blood work was performed daily to assess the trends of my liver function. This was a critical time and my first experience with a post-surgery complication. I had to take heavy antibiotics because I was full of infection from the bile and whatever other toxins were leaking into my belly.

My hospital stay was a real grind. Daily blood counts were discouraging at times; trends were not always favourable. I found myself fighting with all I had but it still wasn't enough. The pain meds certainly took their effect on me too. I would be on the phone with Trev, Sandy, or Ken Loscerbo and all of a sudden I would be describing how I had been making capocollo sandwiches behind my liver that afternoon. I was really losing it.

I was forced to refocus about seven days into my stay. One on-call physician stopped in to see me, telling me that my fluids were a concern. He said if I didn't pee into one of those blue collectors by midnight, they would be forced to insert a catheter. My reaction: "No fucking way." That was the newfound burst of energy I so desperately needed. There was no way I was going backwards on this hospital stay. My experience with catheters had been relatively unpleasant but in each case I was put under before the contraption even touched my body. The thought of going through that while awake scared the shit out of me. I was determined to avoid this horrendous experience and thankfully I managed to nearly fill the blue pee jar before midnight. "Ha! I got this," I thought.

Two weeks into that hospital stay, the doctors made the call that enough infectious fluid had pooled into the base of my abdomen that an intervention was needed. The solution sounded reasonable when they first pitched it to me. The plan was to put in an external drain via the CT machine so that the toxic fluid could be extracted from my body. That certainly made sense to me. I had no interest in carrying around a pouch of gross infectious fluid in my gut. What wasn't clear to me was the method through which they would perform this extraction. The physician's plan was to insert a needle through my back, puncture my liver, and then reach the area full of fluid to begin draining it. The needle would lead the catheter tube that was expected to collect the toxic pool of bile. They needed to take me in and out of the CT scanner a number of times to see how the needle was positioned.

It sounded logical enough. Unbeknownst to me, however, there was no plan for pain management. Holy shit, was it painful. Sara could hear me screaming from outside the room during the entire two-hour procedure. It was truly the most painful experience I've ever had.

I left with a plastic bag attached to a tube dangling out of my back. This bag was certainly doing its job; it had started filling with yellowish bile and infectious-looking fluids. Great, another drain. It was beyond painful but certainly demonstrated the need to get that shit out of me.

As luck would have it, my parents decided to stop in to see me right as I was getting wheeled back to my room from the CT machine. They insisted on coming to say hello immediately because they were concerned about their parking meter running out. I had been screaming in the most horrible pain for the last three hours and here my parents were delaying me from feeling better because of a fucking parking meter. Their intentions were good, but this was definitely a great example of the fact that the needs of visitors should be trumped by the patient's true needs. All I wanted was to be settled in my room so my nurse could give me some pain medication. This social call became another roadblock between excruciating pain and the relief I had been seeking for several hours.

Sara had my back. She said, "I will pay the parking ticket. You cannot see him now. It's not an option. He needs medication right now." I can't say for sure what type of pain meds they shot me with but I was so pleased to be settled. I just can't stress enough the importance of being respectful of a patient's true wishes. It's not about making you feel better. It's about the patient. I encourage people to truly reflect on why you're visiting a friend in the hospital. Is this for you? Is this to make you feel like you did something good? If so, skip it. Do what's best for the patient.

The next morning when Sara showed up I was sitting in a chair, still with the drain sticking out of my back. She looked stunned. She thought she was looking at a zombie. I was so exhausted; I hadn't slept the entire night. Sara paused and had to regroup. Although I was in the hospital, there was no help available. Sara felt helpless and concerned that something more needed to be done to fix the infection and my pain. When she got to work that morning after her short visit, she called Mike Ludwick. She knew he could stomach the scene she had just witnessed. This was not a social call; it was a call to action in a situation that was not for the faint of heart. Mike showed up within the half-hour and Sara met him back at the hospital. They went into problem-solving mode and talked to a hospital administrator to get an alternate plan together for my comfort. Sara then went off to work and Mike sat with me, as he often did. He helped boost my spirits and distracted me from the terrible situation I was in. As it turned out, the hospital team was able to find a more suitable room for me in the burn unit of the hospital. Within hours I was moved and set up in a private room that had a full recliner for me to sleep in. The room change, but also the visit from Mike, was a godsend in my desperate time of need.

Although this was a horrible experience for all involved, the infection reminded me how grateful I was for the medical professionals working on me. The nursing staff and hospital administrators (including the charge nurses) have been incredible. Even in dire pain I always make it a point to remain kind, polite, and respectful; these people really do have tough jobs. I always call each person by name and thank them for even a minor pillow adjustment or response to a request. Extending gratitude is my approach and I truly feel that contributed greatly to my move to the burn unit and the positive energy that surrounded my healing process.

CHAPTER 5
CELEBRATE AT EVERY CHANCE

Brian De Filippo, Trevor Fridfinnson,
Darren Cosentino and Mike Ludwick

"Darren loved to celebrate. He knew how to party and had a particular specialty in birthdays. Even on his own fortieth birthday, he drew us together for a classy, private, chef-catered event. Darren made sure that my forty-fifth would be memorable by arranging a surprise day of partying and fishing. There were so many laughs. I'll never forget how special he made me feel. The energy he put into me was remarkable, almost unbelievable, and he did that kind of thing over and over again. It was the best birthday of my life. I'll never forget it."

–Mike Ludwick, friend

Despite having narrowly survived one of the greatest risks possible from a liver resection, we stuck to our plan for another liver surgery. This includes signing up for having my abdomen opened up again, with a portion of my liver removed. We had to follow through with our game plan of how to eradicate the disease. Our view remained that as a patient, YOU are in control of medical decisions. They are scary and come with consequences but these decisions are yours to make. When you approach them with the attitude that you are part of the process and part of the success, you stay invested. No finger-pointing, no blame, just thanksgiving. Thanksgiving for having the shot to take, the competence of the physicians, and the care of the nursing team. I made sure I always exhibited my thanks despite some shitty outcomes. As Dr. L. would say, "This is medicine, not science."

After my second liver surgery, in January 2012, we were released from the hospital with no drain, no complications, and eight weeks of chemo-free, treatment-free, surgery-free vacation time. At the end of March, we went back to see our oncologist for the follow-up CT scan and for the first time in a year and a half I was pronounced disease-free. There was no visible evidence of cancer in my body. We were ecstatic! We were so excited that we made Dr. Harris tell us twice. We couldn't believe the cancer was gone! There was a kicker though—I still needed more chemo.

We learned that while there was no visible evidence of the cancer, I still needed to clean up the microscopic disease cells that remained. That would involve twelve more rounds of chemo.

Twelve rounds of chemotherapy means six months of treatment. At that point, I had already completed twelve rounds and my body was really feeling the negative effects. To be told that I needed to match the number of chemotherapy rounds I had already been through sucked. I had to start at square one again and relive an excruciating amount of pain and sickness. But I needed that cancer gone, even the microscopic cells.

There was a new type of chemo at the time; it involved oxaliplatin. This is a type of drug used with a combination of other drugs to make up the chemo cocktail. While effective, it caused neuropathy in the hands and feet. Neuropathy is weakness, numbness, and pain from nerve damage caused by chemotherapy. In addition to nausea and losing your hair, you lose the feeling in your hands and feet. Your extremities, as well as your fingers, nose, and lips, also become incredibly sensitive to cold; anything marginally cold will literally shock you. I could no longer take anything out of the fridge or freezer and I couldn't drink Slurpees—which had saved me from throwing up during previous chemo, and I had another six months of that to come. I couldn't swim in the lake during summer because the water temperature was too cold. I couldn't go outside for any length of time in the winter without being completely wrapped up; anything exposed to the cold felt as if it was being burned.

We got through a really rough six cycles over three months and my nausea was absolutely horrible. The cold sensations and neuropathy got worse daily. Every round of chemotherapy pumped through my body intensified the side effects and after eighteen rounds I was at the point where I was worried I would no longer be able to tie a fishing line because I had no feeling left in my fingers. I kept doing yoga but my immune system couldn't keep up and the chemo started to affect my white blood cell count. There were times when my white blood cell count was so low we had to skip a treatment, which was a huge problem for me personally. I had to stay on schedule with the regimen. I didn't want any extra weeks tacked on. I had to get it done.

With chemotherapy, they knock you down as much as they can without killing you and give you just enough time to bring your health back up before knocking you right back down again. The idea is that they're hitting the cancer as hard as they're hitting your body and the cancer, hopefully, is killed during the process. The entire time you're abused and poisoned. After round eighteen, they started to give me daily Neupogen shots to get me through the rest of my rounds. Neupogen shots are similar to insulin shots, not a huge deal but frustrating, repetitive, and just one more thing I had to do. I remember thinking, "I'm sick, I can't seem to get out of this chemo poison, and now I have to give myself a daily shot. Great."

Luckily, Sara became quite the nurse. She gave me ninety-nine percent of my shots. We watched an outdated tutorial on how to clean the skin, fill the needle, and properly administer the shot. The first time she injected me, the needle disappeared. We thought the needle tip broke off inside me and was stuck somewhere in my arm. After a quick call, we learned that the video failed to mention the retractable needle.

In those six months, as shitty as the chemo was, we hit a lot of big milestones as we simply continued to live. We spent a lot of that summer at our cottage on the lake, spent time with friends, went to a three-day traditional Indian wedding, and I turned forty.

That was a pretty big milestone, from my perspective, and I was thrilled to be celebrating it with the people I loved. There were times when I didn't think I would make it to forty and I'm pretty sure most people were having the same thought. To be diagnosed Stage Four and make it to my fortieth birthday was incredible and we had a huge blowout to celebrate. We had won an auction prize of a wine-tasting and seven-course meal at a wine house and we hadn't used it (because I couldn't drink much alcohol during my treatment), so for the celebration we invited twelve of our closest friends and used the tickets for a big blowout bash.

Darren Cosentino and Shauna Arsenault

Another plus of the poison-filled six months was that my liver had healed from the resections and become healthy again, meaning an occasional glass of wine was allowed. I was still sick from the chemotherapy but if I was feeling up for a drink on my good days at least my liver could handle it. Sara and I love wine and Don Streuber, the president of Bison, had been telling me for more than a year, "I've been buying wine from Napa Valley. I've got some very, very expensive, good wine and as soon as you're ready we want to do a Bison company wine-tasting party at our house." That spring, I was ready.

They planned the party on a Monday night to fit my chemo schedule. We all got together and did vertical tastings of incredible $800 per bottle Italian wine. The night was amazing and an incredibly generous gift from Don. It was as if he was saying, "Hey, cancer sucks. You might not get a chance to do this and we can make it happen for you, so we're just going to do it together today." It was a very touching gesture that proved once again that I've got the greatest support system behind me, which makes the shitty days more bearable.

I really can't explain how absolutely fortunate I have been, even with the chemo. Every two weeks went the same—three days of intense nausea and vomiting, a day of rest, and on day five I would bounce back and be my normal self for the next seven or eight days. I would do yoga, work on the house, and stay busy. My body has always allowed me to heal quickly and regain the lost weight, which I think is one of the reasons I've been able to maintain all my surgery schedules.

If someone were to describe me in one word I believe it would be "resilient." Chemo's a beast, knocking you down without much opportunity to get strong between rounds. You lose weight and muscle mass while your health continues to decline until you've withered away to nothing. I'm lucky in the sense that my body, for some reason, has been able to get strong again between rounds, which is completely abnormal. I believe my body's bounce-back time coupled with my positive thinking is the main reason I've been successful in battling cancer.

But seven months after being declared cancer-free, one month after my twelfth round of chemotherapy ended, another CT scan led to very disappointing news. Cancer was back for the fourth time, which meant I was back on the chemo schedule indefinitely. Unless I could find a surgeon willing to operate on my liver again, I would be on chemo until I died. With fingers crossed we headed to meet with the surgeon.

I honestly didn't think Dr. Lipschitz would operate on me a third time. My liver resection was supposed to be one-and-done. But I knew I had to do something other than chemo. I knew the chances that this guy would go in for a third time were low, but I had to at least try.

Dr. Lipschitz was wonderful. His demeanour and approach to situations was remarkably calming despite how frightening the prognosis usually was. Just thinking of Dr. L causes me to well up in tears of gratitude.

He sat us down and hit us with a new plan of action: we would attack the spots on my liver with RFA. We had another shot at beating this disease! RFA can be done externally if the tumour is in a spot that can be reached with a needle, but with three lesions I needed to be cut open again in the same spot as the two previous times. He explained to Sara and me that they wouldn't know if the RFA procedure would be possible until they had me on the operating table and tried to mobilize my liver. In order to get the RFA needle to my lesions, my liver had to be fully accessible. This meant cutting me open, putting his hands inside me, and lifting up my liver to attempt to get the proper angle for the needle to burn out the three lesions.

We were optimistic and willing to give it a try and he seemed pretty positive that they would be able to get to the lesions. Dr. L's only concern was the possibility that scar tissue from my last two surgeries wouldn't allow my liver to turn. Every time they cut me open more tissue had built up in my abdomen and on my liver.

We booked the surgery and fortunately they were able to adjust my liver and treat it. We made record time getting out of the hospital. On day two I was off pain meds and we were allowed an early release. Yes!

I'm constantly doing whatever possible to get released as quickly as I can after surgery to move on with my life. As I've mentioned before, I hate sitting in hospitals and I go crazy when I'm stuck indoors. After so much time in hospitals the last five years, every hour counts. When you first come out of surgery you have a catheter inside you to collect urine, which, might I add, is horrible. As soon as you have the catheter removed you can start dressing normally again, but you have to get rid of the epidural before they will remove the catheter. I've got the process down to a science:

Step One: I Wake Up.

Step Two: Pain Management. You have to appear to be managing your pain in such a way that they're willing to remove the epidural and switch you to oral painkillers. I never cared how much pain I was in; I would tell the nurses to remove the epidural immediately and I would deal with whatever pain I felt.

Step Three: Removal of Catheter. Once that wretched thing was out of me, I could use the bathroom, change clothes, and walk around without carrying an IV pole 24/7, and have some independence.

Step Four: Exercise. The more I walked around the hospital, the better I appeared to the doctors and the sooner I'd be released. If I could get out in five days rather than seven, I was going to. I would joke with Sara that I was literally going to do a jig when the doctor showed up so that maybe he'd let me go home.

Step Five: Get the Hell Out of There.

From: Sara Cosentino
To: Friends and Family
Subject: Cos Update #17
Date: Monday, December 03, 2012

Three for three today—third liver resection, three lesions ablated.

Despite the 5:45 a.m. admittance this morning, the nursing staff was ready to see the Cos, presenting him with a custom-made greeting card. What a boost of encouragement to the three-peat!

Dr. L pulled through with poise as he explained with clarity how three lesion sites on the liver were treated with radiofrequency ablation. As there was no portion of the liver removed—no drain! What a treat that is, one less temporary appendage. To further spice things up, the incision is an imperfect V this time. Instead, it is more of a slash, representing a creative imbalance. Certain to spark even more interest from fellow participants in yoga class.

The Cos is well set up at the moment. His roommate appears relatively normal (no sign of stab wounds, superbug, or an immediate family that exceeds a dozen). At this rate, he will be walking the halls, catching up with his previous nurses, in no time! He has his sights on breaking free in record time. Once Darren shakes loose of his epidural there will be no stopping him (well, other than negotiating with Dr. L...already reinforcing the five- to seven-day stay). My bet is on the Cos for this round!

Sometimes, my plan took longer than I liked. Either my exercise didn't impress the team enough for them to pull some strings and let me go early or they legally had to watch my levels of toxins for a certain number of days. One treatment in Toronto quickly went from a one-day visit to a six-night stay after a nick in my bowel required intense supervision from staff. I ended up being one hundred percent fine with no septic leaks but legally the hospital couldn't discharge me. By day five I'd been to the cafeteria twenty-five times, I was pacing the halls, and reading at the bookstore using free Wi-Fi wherever I could find it. I went back to my room every six hours for antibiotics via an IV before venturing around the hospital again. I had an IV hanging from my arm but I was so frustrated that Sara and I walked out of the hospital to a little deli to order some food.

"What do you want to do today?" I asked Sara.

"We could go back to my hotel and just sleep there all day and watch movies," she joked.

I was sold. I got my next round of antibiotics, changed into my street clothes, and Sara and I were on our way. The hotel was several blocks away and it was the dead of winter but I didn't care. I just wanted to relax with my wife and take a freaking shower after five days of sponge baths. I took a shower with my arm above my head to keep the IV dry and I became a new man. I was clean, refreshed, and on cloud nine. I felt good and a little naughty from our successful escape so when Sara and I snuggled up to a movie in the hotel bed I got a little frisky. We cuddled some more and before we knew it we were having a little love session. The whole time I was thinking, "I bet I'm the only patient having sex right now. I guarantee nobody else admitted in that hospital is having sex at this moment." We raced back for my 2:00 p.m. antibiotic IV treatment and I had a little skip in my step. I was the man!

Of course I was going to sneak out again. We were living *Ferris Bueller's Day Off*. I couldn't go back to sitting at the hospital when I knew there was a hotel room and real food calling my name. I stuffed my bed with pillows to make my absence more discreet, left a note with my cell number on it, and told my attending nurse I was heading down to the bookstore. Sara and I easily snuck off to Banh Mi Boys to get this pork belly sandwich I had seen on the show *Diners, Drive Ins, and Dives* before we headed to the hotel room for a nap. I felt like a million bucks. I had beaten the hospital that day.

Until my cell phone rang, that is. It was my nurse. I had to pretend I was right outside getting fresh air before changing clothes and running back to the hospital. Turns out the entire hospital had been searching for me. Stuffing the bed with pillows and making an escape was one thing, attracting enough attention to require a continuous page in the hospital was another. "Cosentino, paging Mr. Cosentino. Cosentino, paging Mr. Cosentino."

That nick in my bowel really could have been deadly. If toxins had leaked through the piercing, my body would have become septic and I could have died shortly after. I was lucky to sneak out of that hospital unharmed! Before my release, my doctor commented that I had really dodged a bullet. Sara replied, "You don't know the half of it, lady. If you think this is dodging a bullet, you're not even close." When Sara later told this story to her friend, Tim Nickerson, he put it best: "Bullets? Darren catches them in his mouth, chews them up, and spits them out for breakfast. That's not a bullet, lady."

In all seriousness, one of the most stressful tasks during and after a surgery was updating immediate family members, especially my parents, who don't email or text. When you're exhausted in a hospital bed the last thing you want to do is call your parents and answer their million questions. It was, of course, important that my close friends and family knew what was happening first but it was hard keeping everyone in the loop. I always had to be careful what I said. If someone happened to catch me on the phone in recovery, it was amazing how quickly word got around. I had to be careful that my parents didn't find out from somebody else that a problem had arisen in surgery or, God forbid, a tumour came back. That was no way for my parents to find out.

Sara's mom was a huge help. After every surgery, she would come stay with us to take over my primary care while Sara worked. She helped level out the stress and it was nice having an extra person to rely on. One of the biggest services she provided was taking over communication with my parents. She updated them daily on my healing so they were always in the loop. Sara worked full time during my hospital stays and between morning visits, work, night visits, and updates she was exhausted. Sara's mom not only took care of me, she took care of Sara too. She would bring Sara food and alleviate some of the burden that comes with a spouse having a disease. I loved knowing that someone was taking care of my girl.

I also loved the feeling of getting back to my own life after a treatment. The best place to move forward and take care of myself was my home. I would immediately begin strategizing my next plan of action. I had to be in action to keep myself from the negative thought patterns that naturally arise when you have cancer. If you were to pass by my house after I had a procedure, you would never know what had just happened. I might move a bit slower but you would never guess I was on an operating table eight days before. I'd look like a healthy guy with a slight hunch (from the staples in my stomach); I'd be up cooking, working on the house, and going for mile-long walks. I'd always keep myself moving.

Most people understood the severity of a Stage 4 diagnosis but some just didn't get it. It's a simple reality, not a criticism, that some people don't understand what the diagnosis truly means. God bless them for it, they likely havn't been exposed to such a terrible sentence. It was hard for people who saw me look so healthy to understand what exactly I'd been going through. In two years I had four surgeries, twenty-four rounds of chemo, God knows how many injections, and more than twenty CT scans. That's an insane amount of treatment in such a short period of time. My case was highly abnormal.

When people heard of our side trips, they'd ask, "Don't you have enough adventure going on in your life with all these medical treatments?" They didn't understand that the treatments, surgery, and all that cancer brought were my job. The trips and adventures were my life.

After eight weeks of surgery recovery, my liver regenerated. My scar had healed and our oncologist gave us four more weeks of "chemo vacation." I was healthy and we had four weeks to do what we pleased without having to worry about open wounds or nausea. We decided it was the perfect time to cross something off our bucket list—we were going on an African safari. Sara and I had always talked about it and when I got sick we decided it was something we had to do.

I had been in touch with a safari outfitter in South Africa for a while, so it was easy to call him and begin to plan. It was February and, as luck would have it, the beginning of a four-week window where it was no longer the rainy season. Fate gave us the perfect weather conditions. What were the odds this window would fall right when I was given four weeks off chemo? We absolutely had to do it. We got all our shots and were ready to go. We were on the phone with the safari trip company, booking flights, paying for our three-week safari, planning excursions to see gorillas and elephants and sleep in tents. We jumped all four feet into this adventure. We were more than ready.

Sara and I were very excited for this trip to finally be happening. We sat together in our living room going over our plans and continuously talking about how incredible the trip would be. An hour after we spoke to the company, the owner's wife called us back to ask if we had had our yellow fever shots. We'd had all of the other required shots but weren't aware we needed that particular one. We assured her we would get that taken care of immediately, no problem.

Yellow fever is one of the only shots that need to be booked ahead of time. We called the Disease Control Board in Winnipeg and asked to get the shots within the next two days. We learned that there was a minimum four-week wait. Seriously?! This had to be a formality. I was not missing out on the trip of a lifetime for some bullshit bureaucratic rules. We were right on the cusp of crossing off one of my largest bucket list items and the only thing holding us back was a yellow fever shot. We had friends on the Disease Control Board and we were willing to travel to a different province. We would have flown anywhere in Canada in a heartbeat. Every place had a four-week wait. We were devastated to learn that the culture for the shot is actually grown from the time requested.

In this instance we had to take a loss. There was no way we could go to Africa for the safari of our dreams. We were heartbroken when we realized the trip wasn't happening. One minute we were elated and picking our travel package and the next we were completely shut down with absolutely no way to find a solution. My oncologist later put things into perspective and said it wound up being good that I didn't travel to Africa at that stage because I likely would have come back with something mild. A skin rash, a tapeworm, or a stomach bug would have meant my chemo would have had to stop until I was done fighting off whatever I had picked up. This trip of a lifetime would have delayed my treatment for who knows how long, and we didn't have time for that.

So what did we do for those three and a half weeks that remained? We booked a dive trip to Mexico, Cos-style—we booked a flight and rented a car and left the rest of the details until we arrived. We went off the grid and I was gung-ho on diving and fly-fishing. We found a tiny remote fishing lodge with no electricity and headed straight there. We needed to focus on adventures and get away from the monotony of chemo regimens. This trip was the breath of fresh air that we so desperately needed.

CHAPTER 6
LIGHT IT UP!

Darren and Sara Cosentino

"There is one definitive memory that has stuck with me. When Darren was first diagnosed, he came to my clinic and said to me, "Look, it's eventually going to get me. I want to spend as much time with Sara as I can." His focus was her, not himself or his cancer. Darren was trying to create incredible memories and live profoundly day-to-day while he could. He knew how to live with cancer. He knew how to live. For us that knew him, he carried on as if nothing was wrong."

Sue Zwarich, friend

Early 2013 represented a new lease on life for Sara and me. With three liver resections and a colon resection in the last two years, we were beyond excited for an adventure and this proved to be one of our top five vacations. We took in Chichen Itza, went to Progresso to visit some snowbirds from cottage country, and even made a stop off the beaten path in Xcalak. That is our type of travel. Xcalak is rustic. All we had was solar power and a private palapa hut on the beach. The occupants were a rather large iguana and us. Each day we stayed there we had a personal guide who offered us either fly-fishing for bonefish or scuba diving. What could be more perfect?

It was an unreal adventure. Nobody there knew of our cancer journey. Nobody there needed to know. We were a couple from Winnipeg, Canada, seeking some sun and adventure. It was liberating, physically and mentally. We dove with sea turtles, schools of tarpon, lobsters, and caught numerous bonefish. Sara and I ventured down dirt roads. We crossed federal patrols, drove over large dead snakes on the road, and ate ceviche regularly. Who could have guessed that the disappointing news about Africa would be a game changer that turned out to be incredibly positive and influential?

With MRI results showing minimal advancement of RFA-treated tumours in the left lobe of my liver, we were granted another travel pass in March of 2013 and we didn't hesitate. This time I joined Sara on her business trip to Dublin. I entertained myself by taking a five-day cooking class. I blended in with the students but wouldn't you know it—my culinary skills proved to be at the top of the class! Although I've always been into cooking, my cancer diagnosis really advanced my interest in the culinary arts. I invested in a ceramic smoker grill for the cottage and a sous-vide cooker, among many other cooking amenities. I enjoy having an eclectic palate. More than that, cooking provides me with a positive, productive outlet. It has given me a way to say "thank you" to people who continue to help us. It is a social outlet in a casual setting. From charcuterie to French sauces and my collection of cooking appliances, I eventually earned the title "Chef D."

Had it not been for the break in my cancer treatment, I would not have been able to travel with Sara on her business trip and we would not have shared the Rome experience, nor would I have picked up the cooking course. I am eager to spend what time I have left doing exceptional things. Selecting a five-day, seven-hours-a-day cooking course had great appeal. I picked up some tricks, met people from all over the world, and some of my own techniques were a hit, even with the instructor. Sara is convinced that I left an unfair impression of Canadian men who cook. I shared my love of hunting and my ability to not only field dress an animal but fully butcher it, preparing multiple kinds of sausage and prime cuts. I described our cottage home, riding snowmobiles in the winter, and waterskiing in the summer. The class was pretty convinced that Canadians lived off the land, foraged and hunted for their food, and prepared elegant meals on a regular basis.

We also logged a four-day trip to Rome during this European adventure. We spent many hours walking the historical streets and visiting some remarkable historic sites. My cousin, Ken Loscerbo, set us up with a personal Italian tour guide to make the experience even more enjoyable. We weren't asked about cancer once. Instead, we embraced our role as tourists and took in the sights with a profound appreciation for life. We packed in several remarkable adventures in a matter of months with never a hint that I was fighting for my life.

* * * * * * * * * * *

Upon our return home we were back to a routine of CT scans. Unfortunately, additional tumours showed up in May and further travel plans were abruptly halted. The most concerning tumour showed up on an artery—preventing surgery as an option for Dr. Lipschitz. This didn't deter us from our treatment approach, though. It pushed us to look for more surgery options and we leaned on Dr. Harris and Dr. Lipschitz for contacts. Fortunately, Dr. Laura Dawson from Princess Margaret hospital in Toronto accepted a Skype video meeting with us. With a file as lengthy as mine, it was important that doctors actually saw me before they declined to treat me. I had to show them that I was healthy, excited, bulked-up, and could handle the treatment. Once Dr. Dawson confirmed this, she was up for the challenge. This time, my option for treatment was stereotactic radiation.

We flew to Toronto a few weeks before the treatment for some breathing tests. The tests required complete stillness as the tiniest movement could mean the wrong area would be radiated. With all my practice in yoga and scuba diving, I knew I would ace them. In the first one, I had to wear a device similar to a scuba mask; it plugs your nose and has a mouth guard. After I took a big breath, the mask shut the oxygen off and didn't let me inhale or exhale. There was a release button for patients who panicked or ran out of air—it would open a valve and release air. The technicians who administered the test were very timid and cautious from working with very sick patients; they obviously hadn't worked with me before. They wanted to slowly acclimate me to the mask before they started the test, but I was having none of it.

"I want you to be sure," the technician said to me. "We're going to ask you to put this in your mouth and you're going to feel claustrophobic and you might not be able to hold your breath for very long. Don't get excited; we'll teach you how to do this."

"Can you just give me the damn tube? I'm pretty sure I'm going to be fine," I said.

"No, we want to rehearse this, so please practice first with me."

"For God's sake, just give me the damn tube," I demanded.

He finally gave me the tube and I took a deep breath, hit the button, went into my little meditative state and slowed my heart down. I hit a one minute and twenty-seven seconds before the valve suddenly opened and I could breathe again. I hadn't hit the button yet. I was confused and asked why he stopped; I wasn't done, I could hold my breath for longer if he wanted. He looked straight into my eyes and said, "Our machine doesn't go any higher than that." Ha, that's a win!

The second test was also based on holding my breath. For this procedure, the doctors needed to immobilize my liver mechanically while I held my breath. I was locked down and stretched out on a table while the team used a solid piece of metal and a vise to cinch my abdomen. They had me breathe out hard and hold my breath as they cinched my liver down as tightly as possible. I only needed to hit ten seconds at a time, but I made it to thirty-five. I have to admit it was a bit nerve-wracking for me because I was used to taking a breath first, not starting without any air in my lungs. It's impossible to get more air if you panic because you're cinched so tightly.

My breathing skills came directly from my ability to go into a meditative state that would slow my heart rate. Of course, yoga and scuba diving had deepened my skills. I continued to use these methods in unexpected areas. My breathing helped during treatments and healing by keeping me grounded and in the moment. It also helped when I decided to try spearfishing. I had the chance to spearfish in Cozumel and was told the primary risk associated with it was the shallow-water blackout. This didn't scare me off as I knew that because of my breathing abilities I would be completely fine. It was awesome and I actually turned out to be pretty good at it.

Because I exhibited my breathing skills during the tests in Toronto, the doctors felt they could be more aggressive in my treatment. Typically, they have twelve seconds to hit the lesions with a radiation beam before they allow the patient to breathe again. Since movement is involved in breathing, they have to re-calibrate the machine and re-test, hoping they hit the same spot as before. Because I could do such extended breathing, I would be given the procedure without cinching as long as I passed new tests and held my breath for one minute at a time. This shook things up a bit; they had to create new tests specifically for me and we had to stay a few extra days. We were lucky enough to stay an hour away from the hospital at our friend Rob Penner's cottage, where we had a great time. Sara sang the hit song of the summer, "Radioactive," during the daily hour-long trip to radiation treatment. That's me, Radioactive Cos.

Reflecting on this journey, I realized how little I knew about cancer treatments. You hear about chemo, surgery, and radiation. It all sounds quite vanilla. The truth is, there are so many types and methods of administering treatments. There has been some truly remarkable progress in fighting this relentless disease. Stereotactic radiation was something I initially knew nothing about. But when I was offered the hope that this troubling tumour on my artery could be zapped with radiation beams while I sat in some sort of tube with my chest squeezed while holding my breath for a minute, my response was, of course, "Sign me up, hit me with all you got."

And they did just that. My Toronto friends again opened their homes and cottages, lent us their vehicles, prepared custom meals, you name it.

* * * * * * * * * *

We were excited when we finally had the chance to hunt in Manitoba for the first time since I'd been sick—thanks to that left-shoulder port-acath—and we had such a great time that we decided to visit Sara's family in Wisconsin. Sara's parents, grandmother, aunts, and uncles all live near each other in Shawano, Wisconsin. Her parents lived there, moved to Manitoba before Sara was born, and moved back in 2001. It had been two-plus years since I'd been well enough for us to visit her family and it had been a pretty big bummer for us that Sara couldn't see her family because I was sick. Her mom was always visiting us in Canada and had been such a huge help that I felt horrible keeping Sara away from Wisconsin. The decision to return was a pretty big milestone for everyone involved. We spent three days talking, laughing, and taking it easy with Sara's family before we decided that we would definitely hunt again. Sara's family has always hunted, and they taught me to hunt when we were dating. Hunting with her family is always an adventure. We had a great time in Wisconsin and after another round of chemo back in Winnipeg, we decided we were ready to end the year with one last vacation.

It was a wonderful year of travel for Sara and me in 2013. Despite lots of chemo, we enjoyed an adventurous trip to rustic Mexico, a self-guided tour of Rome (accompanied by an Italian speaking 'cousin', Maria-Stella), cooking classes in Ireland, and several hunting trips. We were feeling pretty good. We knew we had some tumours to deal with in the future but we were feeling positive and we enjoyed ourselves. I felt strong enough for another trip, so we headed to Cozumel, Mexico. After having had such an amazing adventure in February, we looked forward to repeating it. We had no idea what was in store for us.

CHAPTER 7
DEAD IN THE WATER

Darren Cosentino

"Darren said something that I will never forget: "If more people tried the things they were terrified to do, they would realize that they could do anything." He lived that statement and encouraged those around him to do the same. It's conversations like these that are forever ingrained in our hearts and minds."

- Lisa Bako and Mike, Sophia, and Aidan Krak, friends

After twenty-seven rounds of chemo and an amazingly packed year, Sara and I were ready to get the hell out of Canada. We had been dreaming of warm saltwater, sand, and sun, and felt it was the perfect time for a positive reset. Though I was one day off of chemo and still nauseous, we hopped on a plane to one of our favourite places: Cancun, Mexico. Although I knew the travelling would be miserable after a full round of chemotherapy, I wasn't willing to waste any time. My bounce-back time had always been two days and I couldn't wait to be snorkelling and exploring with my beautiful wife, so I put my head down and just got through it. I knew that upon arrival I would be somewhat back on my feet—one night of sleep in our hotel and I'd be ready to take on the world by 7:00 a.m. Take that, cancer.

We arrived in Cozumel in early December 2013 after a flight, shuttle, and water taxi. I was a little hungry and very weak, so Sara found a pizza place (only a mile away from our hotel). I decided that I was all right to walk as long as we went straight home to bed afterwards. I quickly realized I was substantially weaker than usual; I had to stop to catch my breath numerous times on the short walk, but I was too tired to worry about it. This is my last memory of the trip.

Sara and I had planned to go scuba diving early on our first morning. During our walk we decided to skip the dive and snorkel right off the shore instead. We knew of a great spot right outside our boutique dive hotel with a steep incline into the water and plenty of manta rays and lobsters. We had gone night diving at this same location back in February and we knew the area pretty well. Our plan was to go for a quick early-morning snorkel before getting massages on the beach.

I don't remember any of this. I don't remember making the plan, going to bed, eating breakfast—any of it. I do remember a few short snippets of being in the water. Apparently I set out into the water alone while Sara put on her wetsuit. The water was a little bit colder than normal but I didn't mind; I jumped in with my bathing suit, snorkel, and mask. I was swimming about fifty yards from the shore, doing dives to the bottom at twenty-foot depths, and checking out the sea life. When I snorkel, I like to dive without a buoyancy device holding me back from going too deep. If possible, I always free-dive.

As Sara was ready to enter the water, I prepared her for disappointment. "The clarity is definitely not as good as earlier this year. I can see fish but there's no 150-foot visibility like last time. There's maybe 50-foot visibility." That's essentially when all hell broke loose. Apparently, I told her to have a look in the water and when she looked back at me I was facedown. My hands were out and I was in a full-on dead man's float. I wasn't breathing and had no heart rate; I was barely floating atop the water. I was stone-cold dead.

Sara didn't pick up on what was happening right away; how could she? I had just told her the water was shit—I was fine, right? She could see the tips of my fingers flinching and I was clearly just dangling there, but she assumed that my neuropathy was acting up again. Sara held my hand and asked if I was okay before flipping me over. She was completely shocked to see me wide-eyed. I was dead. Something had just gone terribly, terribly wrong and my wife was fifty yards out from the shore with no buoyancy device wondering how in the hell she was going to get me back to shore. Sara is a good swimmer but she is a lot smaller than me and has no life rescue training whatsoever.

Sara struggled to keep me afloat and started screaming her head off. She tried to drag my body to shore between screams. The wetsuit helped keep her a tiny bit buoyant but the situation was a total and complete disaster. Sara could have been dragged under and drowned by my body weight.

There were two groups close enough to help us: a dive boat preparing for takeoff and a caged-in snorkelling tour from the neighbouring resort. The snorkelling guide heard Sara's blood-curdling screams and tossed his red rescue tube over the cage before crawling up the rails and jumping over. He swam frantically towards us and used his tube to keep me afloat as we waited for more help. At the same time a kayaker from shore paddled as fast as he could over to us. Together, the two strangers and Sara dragged my lifeless body to shore.

I was dead weight and the shoreline was a fair-distance walk full of coral and limestone. The three of them were falling over as they attempted to save me, bumping and banging me on the ground while cutting their knees and feet on the rocks. When we finally reached land, they laid me on my back while a fully trained dive instructor rushed over. I had begun frothing at the mouth and my abdomen was protruding, distended because my internal organs had already shut down. These incredible strangers checked for pulse and breathing and found that I had neither. The dive instructor immediately jumped on top of me to perform CPR. I was dead—so clearly dead that it was impossible to ignore—but he didn't give up. Our resort manager, Eva, had heard Sara's screams and called 911 before we even exited the water. The dive instructor manually kept my heart pumping blood through my body until the ambulance arrived. If he had not, there would have been absolutely no hope.

Unbeknownst to us at the time, my heart had stopped in the water. Visualize the situation for a second here. From the looks of things, people were guessing that I had either drowned or had a heart attack. There was no visual sign of injury and nothing that seemed to have caused such a traumatic accident. The situation was very different from what you'd see on television. I was not a drowning victim who had been dragged to shore, given CPR, and dramatically shot up, coughing and spewing out ocean water. There was no cheering or tearful reunion. There was nothing changing in my cold, lifeless body and hope was fading with every second that passed. Bystanders on shore were hysterical as they watched and waited for any sign of life, having no idea of what actually happened. All they knew was that a dead guy was lying on the rocks while a man continued to perform CPR with no sign of response.

The resort was a twelve-minute drive from the hospital. With no oxygen for twelve minutes, even with a first responder working full-time on me, the chances that I would come back to life were extremely slim. My wife was now alone in Mexico, thousands of miles away from any of our family or friends, with no idea if she would be coming home without her best friend and husband. Our relaxing vacation had become a scene straight from a horror movie.

Allow me to backtrack a little. During the rush to get me out of the water, we had a visit from another stranger—an angel, really. A woman aboard the dive boat heard Sara's screams, dove into the water, and was at her side in seconds. This woman's only intention was to get Sara safely to shore. When the ambulance finally arrived and the paramedics started loading me onto a stretcher, Sara glanced to the side and saw the same woman standing outside the resort with eyes full of fear. As they wheeled me into the ambulance, Sara hurried over to silently thank the woman, who had moments before instinctively shown so much compassion. Neither of them said a word as Sara gave the woman a grateful hug. As Sara walked away to climb into the ambulance, she knew she would always remember the incredible connection she now had with a perfect stranger. We would never know her name but Sara could never forget her face.

Inside the ambulance, I lay motionless on the gurney as a female first responder straddled me to give aggressive CPR during the drive. The intense pounding pushed the air from my lungs throughout my body and pumped blood through my heart. With every push on my chest the air coming from my mouth was audible to everyone in the ambulance. Sara sat with her feet framing my head, still in her wetsuit with only a towel to keep her warm. The entire ride Sara shouted desperate words of encouragement at my lifeless body. "You got this, Darren! You got this! We're almost there! You're doing a great job!" Although she was screaming at the top of her lungs, Sara couldn't think about the severity of the situation. Her words sounded as calm as they did during a round of chemo. She treated the ambulance ride like every obstacle we had faced: just one more thing to get through. In the sudden chaos, her mind couldn't begin to comprehend what was actually going on.

The first responder continued to do CPR on what seemed to be a dead man. Let's not forget, it took twelve minutes for the ambulance to arrive. I had twelve minutes of CPR on the beach and another twelve in the ambulance on the way to the hospital. That's twenty-four minutes of CPR on a corpse. After fifteen minutes of lifelessness, most responders would assume that I wasn't coming back and would stop pumping. For some reason, this first responder just kept pushing on my ribcage with all her might, never skipping a beat, with Sara screaming encouragement in her ear. Maybe *because* Sara was screaming encouragement in her ear. She continued CPR as we drove into the emergency receiving room.

Once I arrived in the ER, nurses pulled out a defibrillator and attempted to jumpstart my heart. Defibrillation consists of a therapeutic dose of electrical current to the heart. It's extremely intense and would kill a healthy person but it is the *only* chance at restarting the heart once it stops. The electric shock goes through metal paddles directly into the chest and jolts the heart. My nurses put a paddle on either side of my chest and delivered the shock. No response. They tried again and again. No response. They pressed the paddles hard to my chest and tried one last time; on that last attempt my heart started to beat on its own. It was a miracle, but I was still unconscious. The outcome looked pretty bleak. As Sara paced the waiting room, a doctor found her and explained the severity of the situation.

"We've got his heart going. We had to defibrillate him four times. Now it's time for you to decide what you want us to do. He hasn't had a heartbeat for over twenty minutes. I held a flashlight to his eyes and I can't tell if there is any brain activity. We *could* do an angiogram, which would be the natural thing for a cardiac event. The angiogram may help us figure out what is going on."

"Absolutely. Do it," Sara said, still with no information on why my heart had stopped and facing the prospect that I might be brain-dead.

An angiogram is an X-ray test that uses a special dye and a camera to take pictures of the blood flow within an artery or a vein. It could show the doctors if coronary artery disease was present and, if so, the severity of it. An angiogram couldn't, however, predict my fate.

There was more to starting the angiogram than Sara saying "yes." Because we were so far from home, Sara had to put down a $3,000 deposit before any procedures would even be considered. The hospital had no idea if Sara could cover the cost of the angiogram. She had only the wetsuit she was wearing, as far they were concerned. Fortunately, Eva arrived with some personal belongings from the dive resort safe, including Sara's wallet. Sara immediately pulled out her credit card and started making phone calls to make sure my insurance kicked in. With no cell phone or address book, Sara called her circle of close work friends at Great-West Life. It was virtually impossible to get in contact with a friend from home using a Mexican phone but she kept the faith.

None of our friends were answering; the number was very similar to one from a scam ("You've won a free cruise!") making the rounds at the time. (As if we needed another reason to hate those stupid scammers!) Eventually, she got ahold of a colleague who was able to start the ball rolling. Sara's health insurance is provided directly from Great-West so she decided the best course of action would be to go through hers rather than mine. That way, we would have a team of people we knew personally working hard on my case.

The angiogram came back clear; there were no blockages in my heart and no evidence of a heart attack. The doctor had various theories, including the possibility of hardening around the exterior of my heart that caused something to go awry and problems with my enzymes. Every theory the doctor had seemed unreasonable or highly unlikely, so Sara got Dr. Harris on the phone to discuss other possible triggers or things to watch for.

As she stood in the hospital still in her wetsuit, Sara dialled the number for Grace Cancer Care. She knew that number by heart and was connected to Dr. Harris within minutes. Dr. Harris was exceptionally helpful and assertive, as usual, and she was more than willing to discuss my treatments with the doctor. She confirmed that my cancer treatment regimen had nothing to do with my heart (my chemo drugs do not affect the heart) and she insisted that the doctor look for a different reason for this incident.

Back on the phone with Sara, Dr. Harris got straight to the point.

"Sara, I need to ask *you* some questions. Do you know what you're going to do if Darren's heart stops again? Have you got that figured out? Because you need to have already thought that through before it happens."

"Yes, I know what I'll have to do," Sara answered. "Dr. Harris, do I call Darren's parents? Because this seems to be the time that I would call his parents."

"Absolutely, Sara. You need to promise me that the first thing you'll do when you hang up this phone is call his parents."

It was no surprise that Sara wanted to have information for how to move forward before calling my parents. Since the beginning of my illness, Sara and I have followed a protocol for giving bad news— we always have a game plan. We hate being the bearers of bad news without knowing what the results could be or how we're going to move through the process. We like to be prepared enough to answer the questions we will undoubtedly be asked by the people who care about us. Sara explained her thoughts to Dr. Harris. "We've got the push for insurance going and they've already told me that they can't treat Darren here. The cardiologist said outright that they don't have the facilities to treat him at this hospital. We can keep him sedated, intubated, and in a coma. We can continue to give him meds to try to treat the toxins in his blood but they don't have the facilities to treat him. I'm working on getting him flown to Miami through insurance. There's a good chance that we'll be in Miami either later today or tomorrow."

Dr. Harris interjected, "You have to promise me you'll call Darren's parents right now," she said. "Whether they decide to fly to Mexico is not a decision for you to make. That is not something you want on your shoulders." Sara got the point. If I were to die in that hospital and Sara waited to call, she would always carry guilt from not giving my parents a chance to say goodbye. She had to let them make the decision regardless of where I would be in twenty-four hours. She had to call them. Sara expressed her thanks to Dr. Harris and hung up the phone. She looked around the waiting room and collected her thoughts.

I had been dead for more than twenty minutes. My heart was now beating on its own, which was a huge milestone, but it looked like I might be brain-dead. My internal organs were certainly not going to restart properly after not functioning for so long. In a matter of hours, days, or weeks, my organs could shut down for good and I would die. There was not a person around Sara or me at this point who thought I would wake up. It seemed medically impossible.

Sara knew she had to contact my parents very soon but she needed to take one critical step first. After asking the nurses to Google the phone number, Sara dialled the office of my very close friend and confirmation godfather, Ken Loscerbo. Ken is top-drawer; he's resourceful and never wavers in his commitments. He's the closest thing I've had to an older-brother. Ken and Sara are a lot alike in many ways: they are both accountants, they are both very practical, and both have sound judgment.

After explaining what had happened that morning, Sara asked Ken for a huge favour. "I would really appreciate if you could go to Darren's parents' house a little later this afternoon. I'd still like to have more information on where we're going to end up but please head over in a few hours. I need you to be at their house when I call to have this conversation. I don't want them to be alone," she said.

"Of course, Sara, of course. I can be in Mexico tomorrow morning. Do you want me to bring Darren's parents? Do you want us to come there? I'm happy to do whatever, just say the word," Ken said.

"No. I'm hoping we're not here tomorrow. I'm hoping we'll be somewhere that can actually treat whatever is going on. We have to get out of here, Ken. Darren's life depends on it."

Sara knew she had to get this figured out but there was only so much she could do. Soon after the talk with Ken, Eva showed up at the hospital again, this time with dry clothes and Sara's cell phone. Eva tried to get Sara to eat but she was too shaken up and could only drink water. This had quickly become one of the worst days of Sara's life.

Between the hotel staff, the hospital staff, the press, and the people on the beach, I was being identified as a drowning victim. This was a big deal. A foreigner visits the beaches of Cozumel and drowns while his wife is out in the water next to him. Sara tried explaining to anyone who would listen that I did not drown, but in all the uproar, her point was lost. Because of the severity of the situation, the Mexican government decided it would be comforting for Sara to have an armed police officer accompany her in the hospital. A uniformed officer with giant AK-47 walked beside Sara to "comfort" her. I'm not sure that did the trick but the act of kindness directly from the government was much appreciated. Sara knew that these strangers were doing whatever they could to console her in her time of need.

After a battle between the hospital and our insurance company, Sara was ecstatic to receive confirmation that Trinity Air Ambulance would arrive to transport us to Miami around 8:00 p.m. She was full of hope as she made her way back to the hotel to collect our belongings and make the dreaded call to my parents. Eva proved invaluable once again as she brought a laptop and satellite phone to our room for Sara to use. (Our Canadian cell phones had horrible reception in Mexico and they both knew the call would be hard enough without adding potential difficulties like the call cutting out.) As Ken sat with my parents in their home in Winnipeg, Sara explained what had happened. She stressed that the doctors were doing everything they could and that we'd be flying to Miami that evening. Sara made a couple other calls, too—one to her parents and one to Sandy.

Once the weight of telling our loved ones about the tragedy that had just ensued was off her shoulders, Sara took a shower to rinse the saltwater off her skin and out of her hair. "Okay," she thought to herself, "You are where you are; now you need to let this go. What has occurred is down the drain. From here it's all about going forward. Just put one foot in front of the other and progress to the next step. You can get through this." She took a deep breath and exited the shower to tackle her next step.

She left my favourite leather Crocs sitting on the beach. We had two roller bags and a backpack and had been told that there would only be room for one person's luggage in the air ambulance. She had to carry our luggage on her lap and the Crocs were the least of her worries. They were the last thing I needed in a coma, right?

After a long day, many phone calls, and a $55,000 bill for twelve hours in the hospital, the American medics burst onto the scene. It was straight out of a movie. They were trained specifically for these types of instances and they brought everything they needed into the room before re-intubating me. Finally, at 12:30 a.m., Sara and I were life-flighted out of Mexico and on our way to Miami to get more information on what the hell was wrong with me.

CHAPTER 8
AWAKEN

Peter Jessiman, Paula Napier, Darren Cosentino,
Sara Cosentino, Mike Ludwick, Rob Penner.

"Darren had a unique ability to make me feel special and that I matter. Often when I would walk into a room he would say, "There she is" or "There's my girl." Throughout my entire time at Bison he would refer to me as his "go-to" person. That might seem small or insignificant but it wasn't to me. Darren had extraordinary standards and to know that I was a person that he relied on meant a lot to me. Darren has taught me to always take a moment to tell someone they are important; you never know the difference it will make in their life."

Paula Napier, friend

I wish I had been conscious to experience the air ambulance ride to Miami. It was on a small Learjet that looks like a rocket. It's pretty awesome from the outside. The inside was bare, though, with just enough room for two pilots, two ER nurses, an ambulance bed, and a single jump seat in the back for Sara. I was barely alive and had tubes stuck inside me to breathe, my head supported, and my arms bound to the gurney so that I wouldn't wake up mid-ride and rip my tubes out.

I'm so lucky to have a wife like Sara for many reasons. She has an incredible ability to handle situations with as little emotional involvement as possible and get the job done. It's unbelievable to me. Any other person would go crazy in her situation. If the roles were reversed I would have been running around like a chicken with its head cut off; Sara has the ability to focus on what needs to get done. She figures out exactly how she needs to accomplish things and immediately starts working, no emotion required. She called everyone, got our insurance working, packed all of our stuff at our hotel, and had us transported to Miami all on her own.

The official diagnosis of what happened to me on the beach was that I experienced sudden cardiac death and was technically dead for more than twenty minutes. I was in a coma when I arrived at the hospital in Miami. I did partially wake up once on the ambulance ride from the airport to the hospital in Miami; I made a little movement, which was a really wonderful sign.

At the Miami hospital, the attendants rattled off readings based on my toxin levels; they were staggering. When your inner organs shut down, all the body parts that purify your blood, including your liver and kidneys, completely stop working and your body starts to fill with toxins. My organs were shut down for twenty minutes, so there was toxic waste poisoning my body. That's not good for a healthy person but it's extremely dangerous for someone who has had as many liver resections and treatments as me. Sara started to worry about my liver and my bilirubin counts (three different readings taken from your blood that indicate different types of liver problems). Because of my health history, my bilirubin counts were not good leading up to my sudden death, and the added stress to my liver was also a concern.

"Kidneys are what we're worried about here," the doctor explained to Sara. "The kidneys are the mother organ. They're the first thing to shut down and the last thing to restart. Your husband needs to see a nephrologist immediately. If we can get the kidneys working again, that's the first step. If we can't, well, nothing else is going to follow."

On that first day in Miami, a neurologist, a nephrologist, a cardiologist, an oncologist, and a psychologist visited me. I was the most popular guy in that hospital and I wasn't even conscious! I started making some movements, which completely shocked everyone, but there was still not much hope for me. Once Sara realized how lengthy the process was going to be, she decided to find a cheap hotel to wind down and take a shower. It wasn't until around 8:00 a.m. the next day that she was able to take a short break. Still pumped with adrenalin, sleep was the last thing on her mind. Unfortunately, the Miami version of "cheap" was $200 and Sara didn't even end up sleeping in the room. She made it back to the hospital within sixty minutes of leaving. As she walked through the hallway, she saw my ICU nurse, Angel, looking very flustered. Angel said frantically to Sara, "I swear I only left him for ten minutes!"

"Oh shit, what does he mean? He's confessing; I don't know why he's confessing… What the hell is going on?" Sara started to worry as she walked into my hospital room. She stopped short. There I was sitting up in bed with a shit-eating grin on my face. I had an oxygen tube through my nose but I was no longer intubated. Sara quickly realized that I had self-exacerbated. That is, I ripped the tube out of my throat, despite having been strapped down with mitts on my hands just an hour ago.

When Sara saw me sitting up in bed, she recognized a little spark in my eye and knew she had me back. She didn't know how I was going to be or what motor skills I would regain but she knew that somewhere inside me my old self was there, sitting in bed smiling, proud of myself.

I was only in a medical coma for a day, but I was in a delirious state from a lack of oxygen for the majority of my hospital stay. I don't remember a lot from those six days in the hospital but I do remember pulling my mitts off. I remember waking up and looking at the mitts wrapped around my hands and knowing that there was something uncomfortable in my throat. I remember somehow getting my hands together and just ripping the mitts right off. I don't remember pulling the tube out of my throat but I imagine that it was a natural instinct—there's something bothering my throat so I'll just pull the fucking thing out. I remember thinking, "Okay, I don't know where I am or what is going on but at least I know that I'm awake now," before slipping back into unconsciousness.

I couldn't speak for the majority of my stay so when I woke up I subconsciously began making up a story about where I was and how I got there. The last thing I remembered was being in Mexico; how could I suddenly be strapped down? There were strange faces entering and exiting my room every fifteen minutes and poking and prodding of my body. From my bed I could see the hotel logo, a swirled blue wave. The next thing over was a whiteboard with Angel's name on it. Naturally, my mind went back to Mexico and the Blue Angel dive hotel. Bits and pieces came together in my mind and exploded into an elaborate situation where I'd been abducted by aliens and held hostage at the Blue Angel. I was strapped to the hospital bed so tightly that I was in physical pain and I was too weak to move at all. I started to go crazy, wondering why the Blue Angel would abduct me. What had I done to them? Why would they do such a horrible thing to me?

I can't even describe how fucked up my brain was at that point. I was in an ICU psychosis. Lacking sleep, over-stimulated from loud beeping and bright lights, my brain started playing tricks on me. I have some friends in the medical profession who explained that these hallucinations were caused by brain swelling. Lack of oxygen makes the brain swell and puts pressure on different lobes, resulting in delusion and hallucinations.

Sara fell asleep in a crappy chair in my hospital room that night. When she woke up, I was a little more responsive but still acting weird. I would grab her hand, I wouldn't let her leave the room, and I was constantly humming. I've always played with Sara by singing "Sweet Saraline" to the tune of the Neil Diamond hit "Sweet Caroline" and that was the song I hummed to Sara all morning. Sara's mom arrived in Miami later that day and played Neil Diamond on her iPhone for me to hum along with. Sara claims it was super-cute but I don't remember. I fed myself cookies and once I could speak I asked the same questions repeatedly: "Where are we? How many dives did we do?" The staff was absolutely floored when I was able to correctly answer the question of who the president was. "Stephen Harper is our prime minister," I said.

The third day in Miami I awoke a completely different person. I was paralyzed. It was the most terrifying thing I've ever been through. I knew I was out of the coma and getting better and I remembered answering the president question correctly and being happy with myself for that. Sometime during the night, I was looking at the hospital wall and something awful clicked inside my brain. Suddenly, my tongue started ticking like a clock inside my mouth. It began swirling around like the second hand and I absolutely could not get it to stop. I had hypnotized myself out of reality, or so I thought. My tongue became raw and I could not stop, although I knew it was my own doing. I tried to talk myself out of this hypnosis internally. "Darren, get out of this state. If you don't snap out of this you're done. You're done. You will become a vegetable." I couldn't move my arms, I couldn't open my eyes, and I was wide awake going insane but I couldn't do anything about it. I was afraid that I would never wake up from the living hell inside my mind and I would be trapped inside a useless body only being able to hear and think. After what felt like hours—long, miserable, panicked hours—Sara left for a minute and when she returned every alarm in my room was going off.

I had decided that I was going to kick, punch, spit, and bite my way out of this catatonic state and I did everything I could to physically break out. Two nurses and Sara tried to hold me down while I punched and kicked everything in my vicinity.

At 4:00 a.m. I started to snap my legs to get the lights to turn on and suddenly I was the Hulk. I was spitting and swearing at everyone, including Sara. I have no recollection of this. Finally she decided it was enough and told a nurse to medicate me. They had been reluctant to do so previously, as they were very concerned about checking my brain function—meaning no sedatives—but when there was real fear that I would physically hurt somebody in the hospital, they had no choice. I was a violent beast spitting across the room, far different from the sweet loving guy from the day before.

The drugs helped and I calmed down enough to ask Sara to Google "'jokers are wild" and "clocks" for me. I was afraid to fall back asleep for fear of falling back into the catatonic state and I needed answers. I begged her to call my friend Bruce Coombs, a psychologist, to figure out how I had accidentally hypnotized myself and what it meant. She left the room to take a shower at the hotel and make the call.

Within an hour she was back and I was up using the washroom. I had convinced an innocent nurse—who luckily hadn't felt my wrath the night before—to close my curtain and move some things around so that I could easily walk to the washroom. I was hooked up to eighteen different machines, so I got to work right away. I unscrewed IVs from both arms, took off my heart and pulse monitors, and removed my blood pressure monitor. I was surprised at how crazy sore I was when I rolled to my side, leveraged the bed for strength, and rolled myself to my feet. I wasn't the most stable but I did it. The nurses were livid and directed their frustration at Sara, who stood there staring at me in disbelief. I was walking! Her husband was moving and things would be okay.

Soon after that my room got very busy. Physicians, a physiotherapist, an occupational therapist, and nutritionists were lined up outside my room to see me. I was still not sure what had gone on. In my mind, I'd had a heart attack and had been healing in the hospital for a few days. I was okay, though, I was eating and walking so everything was good. I was ready to go home; could we wrap this up, please? I had no idea that I had been dead for twenty minutes. I had no idea that the prognosis at the time was that I would be brain-dead and disabled both mentally and physically. I didn't know the odds of surviving a sudden cardiac death are less than one percent. I certainly had no clue that the odds of surviving a cardiac death without oxygen, having chest compressions for twenty minutes, is next to nothing. It is medically impossible. Well, almost.

Without that knowledge, the questions I was being asked by the staff seemed ridiculous.

"Mr. Cosentino, can you move your toes for me?" a therapist asked.

"I just went for a walk so of course I can move my toes. Why are we having this conversation?" I was a little cocky with them because I just didn't get it.

They figured I was starting all over again from square one. They assumed I needed to learn how to swallow and wipe my own butt again, which typically happens with people who've suffered a stroke. What had happened to me was far beyond that.

The cardiologist finally explained to me what exactly had happened. I had experienced an electrical malfunction of the heart. My heart had stopped beating normally and went into a flutter of three hundred beats per minute, not pumping blood. I had an electrical synapse in my body, which was why they were able to bring me back to life, but my heart was so out of rhythm that it couldn't physically pump blood. I was not dead per se because of the electrical synapses, but my body wasn't working. My organs were not getting blood and therefore weren't working.

Although my hospital stay in Miami was relatively brief, I did make some very deep and meaningful connections, with one cardiologist in particular, Dr. Azur. He was relatively young, judging by his six-year-old son, who tagged along on his Sunday afternoon visit to see me. Dr. Azur had an incredibly empathetic yet competitive style; he was "in it to win it" for the patient. He spent extra time with me, understanding my journey to date and often remarking at how incredible the Canadian health care system had been in treating my disease. He was a pleasure to chat with and always went the extra mile. Deep into the night, he tirelessly researched defibrillator device options that would withstand an MRI test, just hours ahead of the surgery to implant the device. He was also accessible by text, at anytime, which came in handy. When I developed an exceptionally large tire-sized swelling around my abdomen, I texted a picture of it to him and had a response within moments.

After hearing our story, the doctor was amazed. He agreed that I shouldn't be alive. You just don't get as many chances as I've gotten, especially with sudden cardiac death. I wasn't supposed to live through that, but I did. Somehow, I survived. And now, against my will, I had to add a defibrillator to my collection of internal apparatuses. Although I fought it, I wouldn't be permitted out of the hospital unless I had the surgery to implant the defibrillator. Without a reason why my heart had had an electrical malfunction, they weren't allowed to let me leave without giving my heart a way to restart itself.

Two days later I was prepped for my defibrillator implant. The gurney ride to the surgery room was quite interesting. Nurses paraded me around the hospital to show me off to five nurses and a physiotherapist who had seen me days before in paralysis. They were shocked and took turns wheeling me around, saying things like, "Is this the same guy that was in the ICU? I cannot believe that you're even awake, never mind coherent and talking to us." It was a miracle that I survived with my brain intact.

The operation went smoothly. I was sedated but awake for the whole thing and it was done before I knew it. The doctor had called the night before my surgery and asked Sara if we wanted to test the ventricular defibrillator immediately after the surgery. They explained to us that to test the device, they needed to re-enact what had happened on the beach—they needed to stop my heart.

Sara and I were a bit shocked at this question. Every medical professional we had seen had told us there was virtually no chance my heart would stop again. This was a one-in-a-million freak accident, an electrical malfunction. If it happens once, the chances it reoccurs are slim to none. I didn't have heart disease, my heart was healthy, and the whole incident was a horrible fluke. We were not even close to getting back to normal life yet. Why would we voluntarily stop my heart again? We politely declined.

They tested the leads after I healed and everything looked good, another small win in our book. That was until the doctor wrote me twelve different prescriptions. Bring on the side effects! In all seriousness, I was ecstatic to get out of the hospital and back to my regular life. I was so ready for this insanely scary chapter to be closed permanently. The nurses showed up to my room with a wheelchair, as per my insurance policy, but the Cos was not interested in being wheeled out of the hospital. "Not today!" I told the attending staff before I walked out of the hospital. They watched in disbelief. Sara carried my bags just to err on the side of caution.

We spent about a week in Miami before we headed home, but not by choice. The doctors couldn't approve us leaving the city and flying back to Canada until I had healed for seven days. We rented a room at a resort, filled our giant order of prescriptions from Walgreens, and relaxed on our balcony. I remember talking to a friend about our stay and saying, "If I wasn't sick, I would hate it here. If I hadn't just died you would never catch me lounging at some fancy resort. I'd be out doing things if I wasn't in such bad shape." My heart was no longer a worry but I had a giant fat-tire-like swelling in my abdomen from the internal bleeding and compressions. Everything was sore. My ribs were broken from the compressions.

From: Sara Cosentino
To: Friends and Family
Subject: Cos Update #27
Date: December 21, 2013

Cos survives SCD and comes home with some new body armour! An adventure of a lifetime...

Before I begin, please know that Darren is now back at home in Winnipeg, recovering extremely well—truly a Christmas miracle.

On the first day (Friday, Dec 6) of our vacation in Cozumel, Cos took to the water for some snorkelling. It took some convincing that we should wait a day or so before getting onto a dive boat for scuba. That was an excellent call.

A few minutes into our light swim, Darren suffered SCD (sudden cardiac death). No warning—an electric "shut off" of the heart function, so to speak. First responders from the dive shop and neighbouring resort worked quickly to assist with the water retrieve. My constant screams prompted the resort to call for an ambulance in good time as well (Eva and the Blue Angel Resort operated in textbook fashion).

Within a few minutes Cos was pulled from the water and CPR was underway. A physically fit female ambulance attendant continued CPR until we arrived at the small hospital in Cozumel. Receiving physicians paddled Darren four times to trigger a heartbeat. Despite Darren being in a coma, with assisted breathing, and concern for brain damage, the cardiologist continued to do all the tests he could. This included an angio, which came up with zero blockages. With a competent insurance case manager pushing for action, events progressed to having Cos Lear-jetted to Miami via air ambulance within fourteen hours of the incident.

In Miami the prognosis continued to improve. Cos was out of the coma and decided to pull out his respiratory tube by Saturday night. A barrage of tests were ordered by neurologists, oncologists, cardiologists, nephrologists, electrophysiology cardiac specialists, physiotherapists, a psychiatrist (yes...an interesting experience with ICU psychosis), a specialist in swallowing...the list goes on. All tests came back with favourable trends. Organs, including the kidneys, liver, and heart, were getting to near-normal readings and there were no signs of brain damage. Cos exhibited such remarkable strength that by Thursday he was under the knife to have the Cadillac of internal defibrillators (an AICD) implanted in his right chest. By Friday, a week from the incident, I broke Darren out of the hospital with the promise to stay in the area and fill and administer seven different prescriptions. In typical Cos style he resisted the wheelchair and nurse escort to the main hospital entrance. It took negotiation to keep him from dragging his own luggage! A remarkable superhero.

Recovery continued in Fort Lauderdale, in an oceanfront hotel room. Cos enjoyed the sound of the ocean and the opportunity for more sunlight in the room. However, in classic Cos character, he remarked, "if I was healthy, I would hate it here. Disneyland for American tourists." At that point I knew for certain...Cos is back. In fine form.

We arrived home this past Thursday night (Dec 19), two weeks from when we left. A special thank you to Rob and the Bison family for their exceptional surprise visit to Fort Lauderdale. What a way to conclude our "vacation"!

So wonderful to be home—despite the cold. Next up will be additional tests next week with local physicians, who will be monitoring the situation. For now, we take this weekend to rest in the comfort of our own home. Thanks to Lisa and Mike we have enough food to get us through the winter!

I do want to share a few factoids that may assist you in future endeavours...

CPR works. Learn it. You may just save a life.

Ambulances in Mexico do not carry defibrillators...so...back to CPR—learn it.

Convenience stores in North Miami sell alcohol and tobacco products and it is normal to see clerks behind bullet-proof glass. Avoid them at night.

It takes one hour and forty minutes gate to gate to get from Cozumel to Fort Lauderdale executive airfield via air ambulance Learjet. Thank you Trinity Air Ambulance for your safety record and for your willingness to host us for a tour before taking Darren home! (picture attached)

FBO stands for Fixed Based Operator. This is essentially an airport hangar/first class services for private jets.

When a Canadian tourist arrives at a Mexican hospital with code red status, it triggers a call from the Canadian embassy based in Mexico City as well as a visit from a decorated officer representing the Mexican president.

Delegates from the Mexican president wear military fatigues and carry sidearms strapped to their legs. This is supposed to provide you with comfort and support. Smile and roll with it as they don't understand a lick of English.

My mom can shuttle food orders, find coin laundry, and is more tech-savvy than I am. Thank you, Mom!

Memorize a few key phone numbers…you may find yourself without access to your smartphone and need to act, fast. A special thank you to Thomas for answering the phone! He then tracked down Nancy, Helen, and Tim to help me get insurance moving and communications going, complete with delivering an iPad!

When a magicjack is used, the phone number may show up as Florida. Answer it. It is not always notification that you have won a cruise!

The red lifesaver that you see Pam Anderson sporting on Baywatch is extremely effective. These are not movie props…they work.

Hot yoga builds tremendous endurance, strength, and balance (mental and physical). It was a key contributor to the Cos walking out of the hospital—no rehab. Thank you, Paula!

Family communications…for difficult conversations, have a plan. Thank you, Ken, for taking time with Darren's parents, and Marti for your accessibility at the midnight hour to research Florida hospitals and continued communications support.

Have your own medical contacts. If you find yourself in the care of unknown physicians, you will find peace of mind by verifying treatment options with credible sources. Dr. Pat Harris (absolute rock star), Tara, and Bruce: You guys provided such incredible peace of mind. Thank you.

Know who will kick your ass when you need it. Sandy, Rob, Mike L.: not a likely cheerleading squad but effective in lightening the mood and pushing for constructive progress.

Enjoy every precious moment. Take the time to dance, believe in promise; prayer and positive energy does bring miracles.

We are so very grateful for your continued support, encouragement, and prayer. We share this news of a Christmas miracle and wish you all the very best of the holiday season—drama-free!

CHAPTER 9
DEATH, AGAIN?

Darren and Sara Cosentino

"The last time we were all together was the Christmas after his sudden cardiac arrest. We had planned to go to the cottage with Darren and Sara right before Christmas, but Darren had just suffered his near-death experience and we didn't think he would be in any condition to go there, let alone visit with us. But true to form, Darren was up for the challenge. It was freezing cold and the snow was heavy, but Darren insisted on going outside and getting on the snowmobile, just to prove he could. We had a great time together and also got to spend New Year's Eve with Darren and Sara that year because the weather was so bad and our flight to Denver was cancelled. I think that was God's way of giving us extra time with Darren. Darren truly was a superman!"

- Tara Crockett (Hakes), friend

Despite the -30°C temperatures in Winnipeg, it was so nice to be home. My recovery included catching up on a few TV series and by Boxing Day I was back out at the lake with some friends. Not just lying around, either. I was out on the snowmobile and made the effort to get a picture of me in five feet of snow. I had Sara send it out to the Blue Angel with specific instructions to share it with the first responders. I was overwhelmed with thanksgiving. Don't get me wrong, my ribs still hurt like crazy, but I was still out there doin' it like I always do.

Chemotherapy approached quickly and served as a reality check. By mid-January I was back on the misery juice. As my ribs were still incredibly tender, Dr. Harris requested a bone scan. In typical Dr. Harris fashion, the scan was arranged immediately. By this time, I was used to all sorts of scans. I had had at least thirty CTs by then, not to mention MRIs and other diagnostic tests. This one was different. As the imaging was done, the interrogation from the technician started. I found this odd, but rolled with it.

Question 1: "Mr. Cosentino, have you been in a car crash?"

"No," I said.

Question 2: "Mr. Cosentino, have you had a nasty fall recently?"

"No," I repeated.

I was getting a little perplexed as to why this nice technician was asking so many questions. "Why are you asking me? You must be seeing something on the scan; can you tell me what is going on?" I asked.

She paused. "No, I am not able to provide an interpretation of what is on your imaging, sir."

This had me a bit irritated. Then all of a sudden it hit me—the CPR! "Is there a chance that twenty minutes of compressions from first responders may have caused something you are seeing on the imaging?"

Her eyes lit up. "Precisely," she said. The technician really warmed up to me after that. She was amazed to hear the remarkable story behind the violent compressions that had had such a damaging impact and awestruck by the fact that I was speaking to her just six weeks after the incident. Without hesitation, she offered to show me the image. As I glanced at it, I could see a distinct white line running symmetrically down both sides of my rib cage. "Cool," I thought. Yes, every single rib, fractured. An explanation for my pain that did not involve the prospect of cancer taking refuge in my bones. What a relief.

Chemo round twenty-eight was a bit of an eye-opener. For the first time, my body had a terrible allergic reaction to one of the drugs. Three nurses came to my aid, including one who slapped my cheeks repeatedly and told me, "Stay with us." Wow, this was new and very unpleasant. Because of this reaction, this round was cut short and Dr. Harris was tasked with finding another cocktail option to battle the tumours in my liver.

Although the allergic reaction was unusual, I wasn't flustered. I left the hospital ready to go on with my day. With the extra couple of hours and no pump to carry around, I decided to make the best of it. The weather was relatively mild for mid-January and I was craving a nice steak. Sara was at home, as she always wanted to be available when I was hooked up to the chemo pump. I let her know that I was driving to the local butcher shop, just around the corner from our house.

I ran from my truck to the front door and started making my way toward the fine meats section when I was stopped in my tracks. I felt a bit light-headed and immediately went down to one knee. This wasn't enough. I got as low to the ground as I could before I saw nothing but bright lights. I was flat-out on the hard floor in the butcher shop. Within about ten seconds, I was clear-headed enough to recognize that I was on the floor. I glanced up to see the shop owner's feet moving to and fro as she pushed a broom across the floor. "What just happened?" I thought to myself. "Hmmm. Well, time to get up." No panic, no drama. I lifted myself up from the floor and dusted myself off.

The lady behind the counter made her way over and asked, "What can I get you, sir?" I was still shaking off whatever had just happened there. I said calmly, "I just need a moment to decide." The lady looked almost agitated. Really? This lady didn't have a fucking clue. She would have kept on sweeping and never noticed that moments before I was a crumpled heap on the floor. Instead of making a fuss I kept things simple. "I tell you what," I said, "I'll take two pieces of the best meat you have." I figured that was the most appropriate thing to do. No fanfare, no dialling 911. I proceeded as if nothing had happened. Once I paid for my top cuts and got settled in my truck, I decided to take the back road home and dialled Sara.

"Hi hon, it's me. I'm just on my way home from the meat shop. Something odd happened when I was there so it would be best if you stayed on the phone with me while I'm driving."

"Odd? Can I just come there and get you?" she asked.

"No, no problem. I'm nearly home. Just chat with me until you see me drive up."

It wasn't until a week later when I was in for a device check that I was told my defibrillator had fired. Holy smokes. I had been expecting some sort of massive jolt if the device kicked in. I had suffered SCD not once, but twice! How the hell does that happen? Let's just say that my appreciation for Dr. Azur in Miami became that much greater. Sara prepared a touching note for him to say thank you for his life-saving call. I was so very grateful for the exceptional support that kept coming my way. Unfortunately, I did manage to lose my driving privileges for three months. Talk about a blow to your independence. This didn't stop me from getting out and showing up for hot yoga classes; I just found myself leaning on friends and neighbours to help get me around. What's another challenge in the big scheme of things?

After two cardiac deaths, though, I hit a low point and began to question the value of life. I'd had cancer for three years, but this was a whole different world. I had been clinically dead. Twice. I started to wonder if I was supposed to come back to life. Maybe it was the right time to go? I had no idea and I couldn't seem to wrap my head around it. It was bad enough that cancer was killing me slowly but this feeling was a bullet straight to the heart. This was the most emotionally traumatic thing I'd dealt with. I was pissed at my body for what it had done. I was mad that it shut down and tried to kill itself. I started becoming introspective about why my body wouldn't fight along with me. I knew that if my body wasn't fighting back, I was done. Game over. I began to question everything: life on earth, why I had cancer, why I was still alive. Since I'd lost my license and my freedom, I could no longer drive to the grocery store or my yoga studio. I could no longer pretend I wasn't sick and that was a huge blow to my mental state. I found myself getting sucked into an awful headspace.

It didn't take long for me to realize what I was doing wrong. I was no longer spiteful toward cancer; I was focused on being mad at my body.

Once I put things into perspective and directed my anger at my disease, things got significantly better and my focus was back on reaching the top of the mountain. I began to appreciate what I had and the support I felt from my friends and think about how I could give back.

My friends always knew exactly what I needed. A year after my SCD in Mexico, I received a number of phone calls, a card and emails from friends wishing me a happy first birthday. People even showed up at my house to drop the odd present off, saying, "Oh, you're one year old today! Ha ha ha!" The celebration was complete with a small party thrown by some of my close friends. The gifts included a sippy cup, a baby bib, and an electronic version of the game Operation. They thought it was quite funny but it was very sweet, actually.

Sara Cosentino, Kristin Ludwick,
Paula Napier, Darren Cosentino

* * * * * * * * * * * *

Sara has been incredible in the way she's balanced being both my care-giver and wife without blending the two. We've tried really hard to keep things somewhat separated; you don't want your wife and lover to be your caregiver when you're going through shitty surgery and complications. She's done a lot of amazing things for me, dressing my wounds and clean-ing infections, but there are some things I just won't let her do. When I'm in the hospital, she's not washing me. My wife is not giving me a sponge bath in a hospital bed. That boundary cannot be broken.

After what Sara and I have faced, people expect her to be extremely overprotective, but she isn't. Sara takes care of me while still cheering me on as I pursue activities and cross things off my bucket list. Although she has had every reason to, Sara has never once made me feel like I can't do something that I've done pre-cancer. She has never once acted like an overprotective mother. Her ability to separate her two roles is only a fraction of her amazingness. After everything that has happened to me, I love that she doesn't look at me differently or question my choices.

Though I had just experienced sudden cardiac death in the water beside Sara, I knew we would be going swimming once spring hit. Water is a huge thing for me. I have always loved swimming and being in the water. When I was first diagnosed, one of my first questions to my oncologist was, "Can I still swim?" There's something about being in the water that grounds me. And I've always taken every chance to encourage others to jump right in and get wet too.

I didn't think twice about jumping into the lake. I think most people in Sara's position would say, "You know, I just saw you die five months ago. You're not going swimming." She's been amazing at never doing anything like that. Instead, Sara said, "I recommend you wear a life jacket."

The first few times at the lake after my SCD, we stayed quite close to the dock. I had worked my way out of the life jacket. It had been a one-time thing and I was convinced I wasn't having another heart attack so we were done with that. I would stay close to the dock to be safe. Then my cousin, Alex, came out to visit. He was nineteen and super-fit and we slowly made our way out to the middle of the lake. While everyone was talking and distracted we kept getting farther away from the group. I looked up at him and said, "We both go. We're going to the other side!" We swam our asses off. Sara didn't scream or demand we come back. Instead, she threw a paddleboard in the water and caught up to us to paddle alongside. Sara would never tell me not to do something, but she also needed to make sure that if the worst happened, she would at least be there when it did.

Darren Cosentino

* * * * * * * * * * *

I'm very appreciative of everything people have done for me and the fact that I've been fortunate enough to live an incredible life. I don't mean just from a diagnosis standpoint; I really feel privileged. I've had opportunities to travel, I've got a huge group of great friends who are very generous in what they do for me. Because of the cancer, people are so giving that I'm constantly receiving support and generosity. It makes you feel funny, you know? I'm always trying to figure out how to express my gratitude and give back.

There was one opportunity after my low point when a friend's son, Jackson, started to take an interest in the way Sara and I approached life—hunting, fishing, and enjoying the outdoors. He had expressed interest in joining us on a hunting trip and once I felt well enough, I took him out a few times. As luck would have it, Jackson managed to shoot the biggest buck of the season! Seeing him on cloud nine like that made me feel good, like I actually gave him something meaningful. This was the fuel I needed to get back on the path of being an influencer.

Long before I got sick, friends would joke about how I was ahead of the game in many different areas. Whether it was Texas hold'em poker, for which I had a tournament-grade table before it was on ESPN, or sous vide cooking techniques (before transportable cookers were available), I was always on the cutting edge of trying new things and innovative techniques. This hasn't changed. I started to realize that I had developed quite an eclectic variety of interests and passions, and many people were keen to learn them. I jumped at the chance to influence and expose others to activities they were interested in. It was pure enjoyment to have friends out at the cottage for the first time and relive my first introduction to such a magical place. I love providing people with new opportunities and experiences. It's a true joy. The opportunity to teach kids to water ski, encourage my seventy-year-old mother-in-law to do one more ski around the lake, or teach kids to shoot guns makes me happy. The emotions I feel during such times remind me of why I'm still here, why the two sudden cardiac deaths didn't take my life. I love to share what I can, whenever I can. After all, I've only given back a portion of the love and generosity I've received.

* * * * * * * * * *

After Peter Jessiman flew to Miami on his private jet to surprise me, I knew I had to find a great thank-you gift. I wanted to do something extra for him because of how touched I was by his actions. But what do you give the guy who has a private jet at his disposal? There isn't a lot I could buy that he didn't already have access to. My first gift was a picture collage from our trip to Miami, full of pictures of us in front of his jet, in Miami, and in the air ambulance. I had this collage framed for each person who was on the plane and threw in a little thank-you note. I think everyone appreciated that gift a lot. Peter's is hanging in his home office.

Thinking back to the day we left Miami still causes me to well up with tears. I couldn't believe they had successfully pulled off the surprise. The Trinity Air Ambulance team was even in on it! They had been tracking the tail of Peter's jet to time things perfectly. Following the tour and pictures of the air ambulance, Lisa from Trinity drove us to where Peter's jet was due to arrive. She hung out with us, keeping us company while she and Sara snowed me with a story about how we were waiting for the gate to open for our commercial flight. We sat there and chatted as though we were old friends. It was early afternoon when I glanced out the glass doors to the tarmac. There was a group of four middle-aged people entering the building, seemingly in slow motion. Oddly enough, they all looked familiar, but my brain was not able to process the reality of the situation. Not until Peter broke my spell did I realize what had just happened. Rob, Paula, Mike, and Peter had left Winnipeg earlier that morning in -30°C temperatures. They travelled cross-country via private jet to come get me. It was surreal. I felt as though I was Vince from the TV show *Entourage*. What an incredibly special moment—one I will cherish, always.

Fortunately, I was able to find a rare bottle of bourbon, distilled in 1965, through my cousin, Peter Cosentino, whose son-in-law owns the largest liquor distributor in Ohio. This bourbon was not available for single purchase; it was sold only by the barrel, but through my cousin I was able to pull some strings. My ninety-three-year-old Aunt Virgie brought it to Winnipeg after visiting Ohio for Christmas and I had Pete's gift—a bottle of booze he could not buy. Anywhere.

I was so very fortunate to join a group of guys in Hilton Head, South Carolina, for the RBC Heritage PGA Tour golf tournament. My friends at Bison made the trip happen knowing full well that I had limited interest in golf but lots of interest in the opportunity to hang out with great friends, share laughs, and call my golf-fanatic cousins to rub in the fact that I was at such an event. Although I passed on the chance to walk the rounds with pro golfers, I did eat the most crab legs out of everybody.

In typical Sara fashion, she encouraged me to take in all experiences. So much so that her message to Rob Penner and the rest of the guys on the trip was, "Have a good time! P.S. There's no limit. Darren can do whatever he wants." A couple days into the excursion, Sara got an update on the trip. It was a notification from Rob that I was a "shitty wingman." We had come across a hot tub with clothes strewn all around it, filled with naked girls. I had looked at Rob, he looked at me, and, as I was focused on getting to the bar, we kept right on walking. Rob was quick to tell me, "You're the worst wingman ever! We passed up naked girls already in a hot tub to get to an empty bar. Not cool." In the end, we had a cigar by the pool and shot the shit.

On this golf adventure I did make a special effort to get a hat and shirt signed by famous South African golfer Ernie Els. Dr. L was a big golfer and, being from South Africa, was a huge fan of the Big Easy. I couldn't have been any happier on the day I dropped off the signed schwag at Dr. L's administration desk. I intentionally picked a day he was in surgery so I could leave it there discreetly. However, I wasn't too discreet; I selected mossy oak camouflage wrapping paper, a reminder of my interest in hunting, an activity that repulses him. I just couldn't help myself.

CHAPTER 10
HIT ME AGAIN!

Darren and Sara Cosentino

"In my forty-five years of adult life, I have never met anyone that inspired me more that Darren. The Cos was fun and he demonstrated that throughout life and his battle. Not once did I ever hear him complain and those that hadn't heard his story would not have known what he was going through. What I did hear was how he was going to battle his cancer and do whatever it took to reach his goal. And he did just that, in a most inspirational way. I tell Darren's story to anyone going through personal struggles. His determination and tenacity in dealing with his cancer is a life lesson we all should learn from."

Norm Sneyd, friend

In late October 2014, another tumour was found on my liver near the hepatic artery. It was in a very bad spot and the Winnipeg doctors warned against going after it for fear of nicking the hepatic artery or bowel. Shortly after, we learned that the cancer might have spread to my lungs. Dr. Lipschitz couldn't risk the operation so our file was sent to Dr. Dawson in Toronto to discuss another possible operation. After weeks of no response, we felt like every door was closing on us and thought we were reaching the end of our battle. I knew I had to do something to get attention and prove I was still healthy enough to handle another operation.

I headed to the health centre to get copies of my scans, but I knew the scans wouldn't be enough so I took a memory stick down to Costco to print pictures of myself from the last year, taken after Dr. Dawson last operated on me. There were pictures of me catching a huge fish, jumping off the dock at the lake, and doing a headstand on a paddleboard. I was basking in the sun shirtless in every picture and looking and feeling healthy. I wrote a letter saying that I wanted to thank her for her efforts and show her what I'd been doing since I last saw her. I got a call from Dr. Dawson forty-eight hours later.

"Got your scans, saw the pictures. I appreciate that. Thanks for showing me what you've been up to. I wasn't supposed to do this; I was supposed to wait for the radiology rounds, which isn't for another three weeks. I'm putting out a referral to a guy who thinks he can get this lesion via radio-frequency ablation," she said.

I am convinced that those pictures were what got their attention. I now had sudden cardiac death added to my already ridiculously long medical history. I knew Dr. Dawson had to see evidence to believe that I was still the same healthy Darren from before. My last-ditch efforts proved successful. I honestly believe that if I hadn't sent those pictures we would have been ignored.

Shortly after, we had a great video conference call with Dr. Jaskolka, Dr. Dawson's contact in Toronto, and we headed out to do some hunting while we waited for more information. The radiation bead deposit is done via an artery, accessed via my leg. He could clearly see I was healthy and he had no concerns about my ability to bounce back from the procedure but he did say that he had never done this type of embolization before. Since he'd been in the general region that my tumour was in when he made the previous RFA attempt, he was willing to give the liver radiation beads a shot.

While the New York clinic does about twenty of these procedures a day, the hospital in Toronto only performs ten per *month*. Dr. Jaskolka explained to us that while the New York office was believed to be better, they were simply more experienced and thus more confident. Toronto was not a "Plan B" option. They had the same technology and the same skills and they could produce the same results. There was no doubt in Dr. Jaskolka's mind that he could get this one. The only problem was that he was going away for a month and couldn't get me in until mid-February.

We were so relieved after hearing this good news. We no longer had to worry about moving to New York for a month. Our new goal was to get through the month without my tumours growing in size—which would be nearly impossible. Holding out hope was all we could do. Time is such a big factor with cancer. As tumours grow, they get more difficult to treat. That goes for every surgery but it's especially true with RFA because the ideal size for tumours is a maximum of 2.5 centimetres—roughly one inch around. If they are any bigger, an RFA needle doesn't have enough margin to guarantee the death of the entire tumour mass. It will kill most of it, but if even a miniscule part of the tumour remains it *will* grow again. I was still below 2.5 centimetres but getting close. It was a risk we had no choice but to take. I continued chemo and hoped that the tumour would maintain its size and I'm happy to say it did.

The real work involved in radiation beads isn't on treatment day; it's figuring out how much radiation the liver can ingest and planning accordingly. The doctors have to know which exact spot on the liver to embolize to create a single path for the beads to follow. This path leads to a precise spot—the tumour. They have to calibrate mathematical formulas based on individual needs before ordering the radioactive beads two weeks prior to surgery. These equations were highly important, in order to make sure that the millions of radioactive beads inserted into my liver did not start travelling through my whole body. Radiation deposited via this embolization technique is nuclear medicine, which is one of the reasons they don't offer it to very many people. It's an exact science.

I've met some pretty great people along my journey. When doctors and surgeons see you repeatedly and know you literally inside out, a relationship is bound to form. True friendships have formed between our doctors and Sara and me. Our friendship with my doctor in Toronto, Dr. Vic, was solidified through sausages.

We first met Dr. Vic in January for the failed RFA attempt and then again in February for the liver mapping. I can honestly say that I don't know what his full name is—he immediately connected with us as Dr. Vic. I was sitting on an exam table in my hospital gown talking with Sara as we waited to get my liver mapped. While we were waiting, a strange man poked his head through the curtains and glanced at Sara and me.

"Oh, I get it now," he said.

"I'm sorry, who are you and what are you getting?" I asked.

"Oh, I'm Dr. Vic. I'm apprenticing with Dr. Jaskolka. I'm a doctor, don't worry, but I'm getting my second degree in radiology intervention. I'll be participating in your radiology surgery. I read your file and thought to myself, 'This is a guy who has been through more things than any human being should be able to.' I assumed you were probably a frail, decrepit, ninety-pound weakling. I did not expect to see someone as healthy as you."

"Really?" I said with pride. "You want to do a pushup contest? Because if that's what we have to play for I think I can beat you right now."

"I think you might be able to," Vic agreed.

We hit it off immediately. We joked and talked about what we did in our spare time. He said that he was Hindu and was supposed to be vegetarian due to his faith but admitted that he was a huge meat eater. Sara and I were looking for a recommendation on where to eat that night, so we asked Vic. He recommended a great steakhouse with some of the best cured meats around, at which point I told him that I cured meat and made sausages myself. I told him, "You know what? If I ever come back I'll bring you some of my sausage. You'll love my sausage."

When we came back to Toronto for the actual liver mapping, my new buddy Vic was the assisting doctor again. Just like before, we chatted through the whole visit. We talked about the Jets, hockey, curing meats, and before we made our way to the treatment room I reminded him of my promise.

"Okay, Vic. When I come back next time I promise I'm actually going to bring you some homemade sausage." He laughed; it was all a joke to him. What were the chances a patient would bring his assisting doctor homemade sausage from a buck he'd shot himself? Moreover, what were the chances the patient would bring said sausage on a plane from Winnipeg to Toronto? I guess he really didn't know Sara and me yet!

Vic wheeled me into the procedure room before freezing my hipbone and putting iodine on the same spot to prevent infection. I was wearing only a hospital gown and to access my hip Vic had moved the gown to the side, leaving my junk out for the whole world to see. I was fully exposed but used to it. Vic used a large cotton Q-Tip to apply the iodine from the centre of my hip outwards. I watched as the brown circle continued to grow. He was a lot more liberal with the solution than I'd imagined he would be and the iodine started to tingle on my skin. When it began dripping down my thigh and into my lap, it was uncomfortable, but I couldn't adjust myself because my hands weren't sanitized. I could feel the solution reaching my junk and three minutes later my entire package was on fire. Vic continued to chat with me, but I could no longer take the burning. It felt like someone had a blowtorch under my boys.

"Vic," I asked, "am I supposed to feel warm down there?"

"Yes, iodine can cause a little bit of heat. It's sensitive on certain regions."

"Vic, it's fucking sensitive right now. Somebody could be roasting marshmallows off my boys right now. I need you to move my junk to the left."

"Uh, pardon?" Vic asked.

"Yeah, you heard me right, Vic. I need you to shift everything. My whole package. I'm sorry to tell you this but someone's gotta move my junk to the left away from the iodine. I'm not going to be able to put up with this."

With a bit of a laugh, Vic shifted everything for me. I didn't like the fact that a guy was touching my junk but you gotta do what you gotta do. The next time I went in, a cute little blonde nurse was the one administering the iodine. I had fun chatting her up before I realized she would have to do the exact same thing Vic did last time. "Alright," I thought, "this isn't so cool anymore." It was embarrassing but she was a much better option for moving my junk and I told her in advance, so I avoided the burning sensation. Trust me, she did not want any part of my junk. She was a nice-looking girl but I didn't want her to see my stuff hanging there let alone have to adjust me. But hey, the iodine didn't touch my boys so life was okay.

From: Sara Cosentino
To: Friends and Family
Subject: Cos Update #35
Date: February 19, 2015

Toronto General Hospital hosts Cos...just for the day this time!

The re-strategizing had us back in Toronto this week. Treatment teams keep coming up with new options for beating these persistent tumours. Cos continues to respond to options with "blast me with all you've got!"

Step 1 of a two-step process for radioembolization is now complete. Step 1 consisted of an angiogram mapping of Darren's liver, complete with determining artery routes for transporting crystals of radiation to the infected portion of the liver. Simple enough?

We hope to have step 2 administered in a couple weeks. Apparently it takes some time to calibrate the amounts of radiation to administer to selected arteries, as well as to team with the doctors who administered stereotactic radiation eighteen months ago. Makes a two-week turn-around sound more than reasonable.

Cos continues to look great, and no doubt will bounce back from today's procedure in a few days. He has even more nurses to charm and is somehow now a "bro" with the attending TO radiology doctor, "Vic." This is despite the fact that every conversation gravitates to hockey—which Cos knows nothing about! Go Jets Go!

We hope to return home tomorrow night and prepare for the next blast.

When our third trip to Toronto in 2015 came around, we were beyond ready to start the radiation. Like the previous times, we flew in a day and a half early. We always give ourselves extra time to avoid outside interference. If we waited until the morning of and our flight was delayed, our whole treatment plan would be screwed.

It was on this day that we met Dr. Jaskolka in person. He is a character. He was completely revved up and excited about doing the procedure. He had a whole plan of action that he was stoked on and apologized for the delay. Little did he know we had been so thrilled about the procedure being done in Toronto and my tumours remaining the same size we had completely forgotten about the month wait. A number of his staff members were in the room to observe the procedure. They bombarded us with questions, making it clear that embolization to the liver procedures were a rarity at this hospital.

Before I went into the operating room, who pokes his head in but my buddy Vic. He wasn't even working that day, but he heard I was coming in and decided to stop by the hospital.

"I had to come see you! I wanted to let you know that I'm not going to be part of the procedure but best of luck to you," Vic said, before jokingly asking if I remembered to bring him my sausage. I reached over to the small locker in my recovery room and pulled out a Ziploc bag.

"Yep. I did remember that sausage, Vic." Although I had had no idea if I would run into him during this particular stay, I had it there waiting for him. As I handed over the bag of homemade sausage, he paused for a moment and shook his head in disbelief.

"I can't believe you remembered to bring this," Vic laughed.

"You asked for my sausage, you're going to get it," I said. (That was a big hit with the staff.)

As I was wheeled into the operating room, I heard hard rock music blasting through the doors. It was a full-on party in my procedure room. The nurses explained that Dr. Jaskolka liked to listen to hard rock tunes while he operated. They asked if I was okay with it. I responded, "Yeah! Whatever! If that's what he likes, rock away!"

Before I knew it, there was a barrage of students walking into the operating room, reinforcing my impression that this type of procedure was a rare one. It seemed that every aspiring radiologist and their dog wanted to see Dr. Jaskolka perform this radiation bead deposit. I had a full audience watching me while I was under sedation, bright white lights shining over my body as radiation ablated my tumour. It was a little bit overwhelming. My junk was hanging half out of my hospital gown and a catheter was going to be inserted into my carotid artery. It became unnerving when the surgeons and their assistants walked into the room covered from head to toe in full lead outfits, the same material that covers vital organs during an x-ray. They even had clear plastic shields covering their faces. Even after all we had been through it felt like I was living a scene from a sci-fi movie. And I was the lab rat.

The precautions were completely understandable. The beads I was injected with were fully radioactive. These people had to protect themselves. It was just strange to see the extent of the protection they were using just being around the radioactive glass beads while knowing that these same beads were going inside my body. Millions of them.

An interesting thing about the beads is that it takes sixty to seventy-five days for the radiation to be fully expelled from the body. While the radiation dissipates, the glass beads will remain in me forever. Even though they're no longer radioactive or of use, they lodge in my liver and become a part of me. As of now they don't have a way of getting them out. How weird is it to imagine that I have a couple million microscopic glass beads sitting in my liver forever?

Just before the surgery began, the team read through a list of steps for the procedure. The whole thing was very regimented and included a legal aspect. Although I had read through the document so many times I knew it by heart, a doctor was legally bound to read aloud the step-by-step list of exactly what they would be doing to me. When the blonde nurse, the same one who escaped having to adjust my boys, finished verbally checking off the steps for the procedure, she announced to Dr. Jaskolka that she was ready to begin. Under his lead, she would be the one injecting the radioactive beads into my body.

"Okay, Dr. Jaskolka, I am ready to begin the procedure," she said.

"By the way," Dr. Jaskolka said out of nowhere, "Darren's got a defibrillator because he had a sudden cardiac death back in December. Apparently it's irrelevant so don't worry about it."

This doctor looked at me before looking back at Dr. Jaskolka. "You're kidding," she said.

"Interesting story, but irrelevant. Proceed," he said.

The poor girl. She had no idea what she'd gotten into with me.

From: Sara Cosentino
To: Friends and Family
Subject: Cos Update #36
Date: March 19, 2015

Radiation…activate

Cos was blasted via radioembolization today (step 2: millions of glass spheres filled with radiation transported via the arteries). The TO doctors took an aggressive approach with their calibrations, going after the right side of Darren's liver. Cos looks great, and is resting well back at the hotel already.

The instructions for the next few days are to monitor for side effects and stay away from kissing babies and hugging pregnant ladies. Neither a high risk for Cos.

Fortunately, Darren's doctor bro, Vic, didn't bring up the Jets' losing streak. He was easily distracted by the homemade dried sausage Darren brought for him. Little did Dr. Vic know that Cos delivers on his promises. The doc was shocked and very impressed.

For those who are curious:

No. Cos doesn't glow.

His bodily fluids do not glow either. (We honestly asked the lead doctor how all that worked. He came up with a very scientific response.)

Crossing the border within the next thirty days is highly discouraged. Apparently, traces of radiation can get picked up by border security and may trigger some very "uncomfortable" searches…

Cos is a legend with the local treatment team. His case has attracted another entourage of students. Also, anyone looking for information on Cozumel seems to scout him out (??).

The glass from the radiation crystal spheres remains in the body indefinitely. Apparently there are now millions of them in his liver. That's a lot of balls.

Given the current favourable trends, our plan is to return home on Sunday.

Thank you all for your continued support and prayers. This journey continues!

P.S. Cos keeps threatening to "light me up" tonight, not sure what he means by that…

CHAPTER 11
CONTROL YOUR DESTINY

Trevor Fridfinnson, Sara Cosentino,
Mike Ludwick, Shauna Arsenault, Rob Penner,
Geeta Sankappanavar, Sandy Burt, Darren Cosentino

"Darren dared me to live outside my comfort zone and inspired me to colour outside the lines of life. He leaned into life and relationships long before it became the catchphrase. I am so proud of him as a husband, son, friend, cousin, and human being. He lived life fully and gratefully and gave immeasurable love and support to all those who were blessed enough to live in his orbit. His mark in this world will always be remembered. He was blessed to have been loved every day of his life."

- Marti Cosentino, cousin

From the beginning we faced this cancer journey with a desire to fight with fierce intensity. We were practical but persistent. Although control of the disease's progression was limited, we would seek options at every stage of the battle. When surgery options were exhausted, it was a tough blow. We came to a crossroad. The decision was either to pursue more chemotherapy, even though it was not producing noticeable benefits and was causing skin irritations and limiting quality of life, or walk away from treatment altogether. The benefits of treatment were no longer outweighing the consequences of stopping the treatment.

My philosophy from the start of this journey has been to live life, not add time. If the time added was of limited quality and at the expense of adventure, time with friends, and moments of laughter, it was not worth it. Sara and I made the difficult decision to focus on living for this stage of the fight. I grappled with this considerably. This was not surrendering to the disease. On the contrary, this was my last big punch. It was to show this fucking disease that I was alive and thriving. This pushed us to travel to Mexico and get back scuba diving. This was a new territory, as I was not only a cancer patient with forty-six rounds of chemo and multiple rounds of radiation under his belt (not to mention being filled with glass beads), but I now sported both a defibrillator and a port. "So what?" we thought, "Bring it on." Even when faced with a shitty deal, we took control. At that stage we chose travel and adventure. We started with several days in Playa del Carmen then went back to our boutique dive hotel in Cozumel, the Blue Angel. Yup, that's right. Back to ground zero.

Keeping in control also involves considerable planning and responsibility. I knew the destiny that I was facing. I was not afraid of death. What I was afraid of was dying. I did the responsible thing by having a lawyer cousin of mine prepare an updated health care directive with very explicit language, including a "do not resuscitate" order. I had Sara carry this on planes, boats, and, of course, the beaches. We were all set for this leg of our journey and I was excited. Not only was this my chance to dive again, it was also my shot at challenging the depths that my defibrillator could withstand and pushing my limits.

This first trip back to Mexico in December 2015 post-SCD was amazing. We stayed in boutique hotels, lived like the locals, went to yoga classes, and frequented markets. It was refreshing. In my typical fashion, after three days I had hit my max of relaxation time. I needed to get back into the water. Not just touch the water, but scuba dive. I convinced Sara to leave our comfortable accommodations despite having additional nights pre-paid. It was time to get back to the dive resort and piss on the site where my heart stopped pumping.

Not until we arrived at the doorstep of the Blue Angel Resort did I realize that the memories there for me were dramatically different than for Sara. That didn't stop her; she remained true to our approach. She's a tough one, I tell you, and we were a team. What I needed and wanted to experience was in sync with the support she had to offer. I would not trade cancer for divorce, ever. If someone said, "I can get rid of your cancer but you have to divorce Sara," I would choose to keep the cancer, no questions asked.

We showed up at the resort and dive shop as if we barely knew the place. I was keen to stay under the radar so I would be allowed to dive. There are a number of liability waivers that have to be signed and there was no way that the dive shop would allow me to venture out miles from shore with a group of gringos in eighty-five feet of water if they knew I was the same "dead guy" they pulled from the water two years before. As hoped, our undercover mission worked like a charm and we spent a few days diving without incident. I felt alive again and I was jazzed up to report back to my medical teams that the safe depth for a diver with an implanted defibrillator was at least ninety-five feet. Ha!

Our visit to the Blue Angel would not have been complete without some very sincere thank-yous. We broke our cover once our dives were done. This started with approaching the front desk to ask if Eva, the dive hotel owner, who had helped Sara so much, was going to be around. The staff was polite but guarded. They were reluctant to divulge information about her whereabouts so I came clean on who I was. The expression on the young girl's face was unforgettable. Her eyes got large and her right hand immediately reached for her heart. She shared that she had been there the day I had "died" and recalled the events vividly. As she spoke, she lunged forward, offering the biggest hug I had ever felt. Sharing this moment with a stranger was so powerful. I knew that despite the circumstances, my choice to return to this place had a profound impact on many others. We embraced for what felt like minutes, followed by a hasty step back as the young lady scurried behind the front desk, reached down, and pulled out a plastic bag. She looked up at me with the bag in her outstretched hand and said, "This is your mask and snorkel. We've been holding onto it for you." My heart melted, again.

That evening we got a chance to say thank you to Eva as well. She was teary-eyed and gracious. We made a point of riding bikes over to the Costamed hospital, where physicians had saved my life. It was nearly an hour ride each way! Now I understood why my ribs were so sore from all those compressions; it was a lot further than I had imagined. We took photos outside the hospital and Sara sought out several doctors to express personal thanks. It was a very rewarding experience. We gave thanks, despite the daunting journey ahead.

We had such an awesome time in December that we decided to make a routine of it. Just four weeks later we were back in Mexico, this time Los Cabos, for an amazing two weeks. I had regained some confidence now that I had a few dives under my belt again. I researched Baja and went back to our style of booking only a car, no hotels. I had a list of must-dos and we knocked them off like pros. Our adventure took us to Cabo Pulmo, an off-the-grid preserve where we dived every chance we had. Whether rough waters or calm, each trip out topped the last. From diving with twenty swarming bull sharks to bait balls, sea lions, and snorkelling with whale sharks in La Paz, to boating with grey whales and swimming under the arch at Lands End, we took it all in and loved every moment. We connected with dive masters on a personal level and experienced more sea life than ever before. I even bought fresh live shrimp off a shrimping boat before I realized that I needed to devein and behead the little critters in a Hilton hotel room. This was certainly not what you'd expect from a typical hotel guest let alone a hotel guest with terminal Stage 4 cancer. I was still fighting and living life to the absolute fullest.

With just one day remaining in Los Cabos, we decided to stay in town and I committed to try a stop at the beach. This lasted about ten minutes. My lack of interest is similar to my distaste for any large hotels or all-inclusive resorts, complete with vacationers lounging around drinking umbrella drinks. Though it was nearly 10:30 a.m., I approached one of the boats to ask whether a dive trip was still an option. To my surprise (perhaps aided by the flash of a few American greenbacks), we were on a dive boat within the hour. No time for lazing around in the sun; there was shit to get done! Besides, if you ask enough experienced divers, they will tell you that an eighteen-hour rest period before flying is sufficient.

The experience in Los Cabos was missing only one thing—sharing. After such a remarkable adventure I returned home determined to share it with as many people as I could. This was not because I wanted to brag but because I wanted to inspire others to get out there and experience something similar. Within four weeks, we booked another trip to Mexico, back to Cozumel for the primary purpose of diving. This time, I was on a new mission: to get as many friends as I could hooked on diving. This was quite a task. Dive certification takes online study as well as technical swimming and equipment skills ahead of open water dives. This is particularly tricky for people living in Canada, especially in the dead of winter, but for my crew it was just a small hurdle.

My buddy Sandy was the first to sign up, taking weekly classes before his open water certification in Vancouver. My Bison friends were not much harder to convince. Mike Ludwick, Rob Penner, Brad Chase, and Shauna Arsenault signed up for pool study. Their commitments for Mexico were overwhelming. This was truly the trip of a lifetime. I felt pure joy being able to encourage our close friends to join the scuba diving community. It was like seeing kids catch their first fish or get up on water skis for the first time. I was fully in control of influencing friends and inspiring laughter. This wasn't about me or my daunting journey ahead; this was about those around me, whom I love dearly. I could have lived in that moment forever.

CHAPTER 12
GOODBYE

Darren Cosentino and Ken Loscerbo

"The recollection I have of Darren that has the greatest impact on me was his calmness and dignity while he faced his death. Darren had no illusions. He was completely lucid and he knew very well what was coming very shortly. The suffering was pervasive. What there was no hint of, however, was bitterness, anger, self-pity, or asking 'Why me?' He was just so grateful."

Ken Loscerbo, "cousin"

Shortly after returning from Mexico in March of 2016, Darren showed increasing symptoms of liver failure. Despite the additional physical challenges this caused, his spirit remained strong. We took on a full kitchen renovation in early April while simultaneously renovating a rental property to prepare for sale. Darren put his work clothes on each day. Some of those days he spent more hours sleeping on the floor of the empty rental than he did renovating it, but he never stopped pushing himself to get things done. His body was failing him, again. Instead of getting angry or remorseful, he welcomed visitors and fought each new symptom as it presented. Darren was very aware. He surrounded himself with those he loved. His desire during this time was to stay at home, close to me, and in control of as much as he humanly could be. His kindness and thanksgiving grew even stronger during these days.

On May 19 we had our last visit with Dr. Harris. Darren was now a week into the palliative care program and he was struggling more and more with fluid retention in his abdomen and legs. His mobility was compromised and he could no longer walk a city block without getting winded. It was important to Darren that he saw Dr. Harris, not because he was expecting a miracle, but because he wanted to thank her and say goodbye. The exchange was deeply touching. The usually feisty Dr. Harris was different; she was soft-spoken and reluctant to provide a prognosis. She spoke to us like a true friend, a friend who was sad. Not only did she share how upset she was, she expressed that the physicians on Darren's team, including Dr. Lipschitz and Dr. Mottola, were all incredibly sad. In the midst of it all, Darren remained strong. He was forever the cheerleader, expressing how great a shot each doctor took. With arms outstretched, he engulfed Dr. Harris's five-foot-tall, slender frame in a loving embrace, one that triggered tears and deep heartache.

The very next day, the defibrillator clinic came out to turn off his device. We had decided that disconnecting Darren's defibrillator was a necessary step. If we didn't do this, it would have jolted him back alive repeatedly when his soul was ready to leave his body. We did not want to experience a harder death than we had to. Darren took this in stride. After all, it was part of the process.

We were still determined to get out to the cottage for the May long weekend. How could we not, when it was what we always did? Sandy made another surprise visit and joined the festivities. He was very helpful with some of Darren's care needs and demonstrated his friendship in many ways. Whether it was massaging Darren's aches in the middle of the night or cleaning up vomit in the early morning hours, Sandy was there. Darren's physical condition was worsening but it didn't stop him from taking the fishing boat out for one last spin, which was priceless. Ken Loscerbo and his son Alex spent the weekend with us, as they often did on long weekends. Shauna Arsenault spent an evening out and Mike and Kristin Ludwick stopped by, along with Brad Chase and his son Jackson. These were all normal activities for a summer weekend at the cottage, but it was hard to ignore the fact that it might be Darren's last. Darren was loved by so many and this part of the journey was no exception. He was constantly surrounded by those closest to him, those who loved him and whom he loved back unconditionally.

I was becoming more concerned about leaving Darren on his own during the day. Although I had been working primarily from home for the last several weeks, I was growing less comfortable with my periodic in-office visits. I asked my mom to fly out, which proved to be a very smart move. By Thursday, May 26, Darren was with the caregivers he was most comfortable with: my mom and me. We had become a dynamic team fuelled by a single common interest: Darren's comfort.

Visits from friends continued but we became increasingly selective about who we allowed over. As the days went by, the engagements steadily decreased and Darren's energy level became very low. Shauna would stop in for the day, prepared for the possibility that she might only interact with Darren for a few moments here and there. Just her presence in the house was comforting for Darren. Even if he didn't speak to her, he wanted her there. The same went for Mike, who would stop in after work to sit in silence with Darren. Ken would stop in and massage Darren's aches and pains regardless of the time of day. These friendships were deep, not scared off by sickness or fear.

Darren's last days were not remarkably different from his pre-cancer days. He was determined to get himself up and out of bed. He followed his routine of coming downstairs for breakfast and functioned as normal as he possibly could. The only difference was his depth of conversation. He was selective with his words and consumption of energy. On May 29, he insisted that I lie down with him and listen to a number of things he wanted to share. This was deep. It was emotional, thoughtful, and coming from a dying man, who had nothing but thanks to express and concern for others. He provided instructions on how to avoid tax inefficiencies, directions for trips that still needed to take place, relationships that needed to be enriched, and care that needed to carry on. Darren was filled with respect and thanksgiving. He was articulate, sharp, and driven despite a nearly lifeless physical body.

The last few days also included visits from various physician teams. They were interested in his fight, his journey, and his outlook. These physicians craved more conversations and time with Darren. They sat intently and listened to him express his state of being. Although it was painful to hear him say that he no longer felt joy, it did bring a sense of peace to us all—peace with the fact that his mental state was in lockstep with his failing body. As sad as that was, it also represented his alertness. Darren's spirit never wavered. His passion for life and mental stamina was awe-inspiring. In the very last hours of his life, he had a deep conversation with our church pastor, Bruce Martin. Then one last massage from Ken. Darren never once complained. Instead he expressed ongoing gratitude: "Thank you"; "I'm sorry to ask this but can you help me move?"; "Thank you"; "I am so lucky, I have the best family in the world." What a remarkable, loving man my husband was.

Minutes before Darren passed, he asked me to call 911. He knew he was slipping away yet still wanted to fight it. His body was paralyzed but his mind was sharp. I give thanks each day for spending those last remaining days, hours, and minutes with such a remarkable human being. We said goodbye, but in a way that acknowledged that we would be together again. Darren told me he would be waiting for me and those words give me strength each day to live as he would want me to. In the early morning hours of May 31, 2016, Darren's spirit slipped away. He left his cancer-filled body to be free to laugh, dance a jig, and swim again.

Darren and Sara Cosentino

DARREN'S TOP TEN PHRASES

1. First one in, last one out.

2. Dare to live, not just extend time.

3. Give people what they want; you will get what you want.

4. Venture outside your comfort zone. If more people tried the things they were terrified to do, they would realize that they could do anything.

5. Make the choice to "be the guy" (get the crowd dancing, convince people to scuba dive, organize the poker party, plan the sausage-making event, initiate the trip of a lifetime, take the shot, book the travel, get the fishing line in the water, paddle, ski, wakeboard, book the dinner party, try the new cooking techniques), because you can.

6. Less talking, more doing.

7. Don't settle.

8. Laugh often.

9. "Wow me!"

10. Gratitude: say thanks, then say it again.

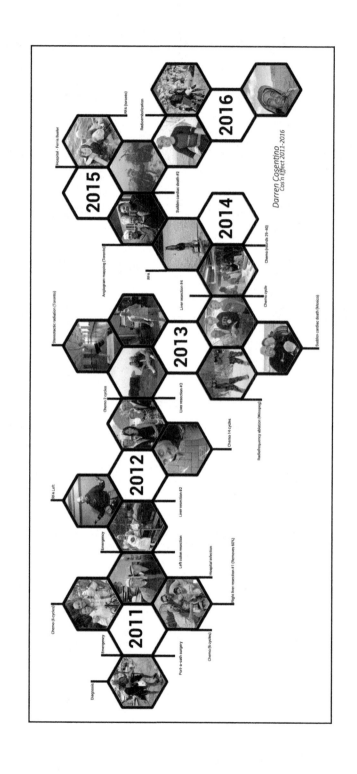

Darren Cosentino
Cos'n Effect 2011-2016